Miniature Quilts

by Margaret Boyles

Meredith® Press
New York, New York

Dedicated to my Sunshine, my granddaughter, Nicole Barringer Eastman, who modeled for several of the photographs.

Dear Crafter:

Whether it's a place mat, a doll quilt, or a small picture, diminutive versions of full-size quilt patterns are more popular than ever. This subject is a natural for Margaret Boyles, a master of heirloom sewing. In Miniature Quilts, you will find a collection of graceful designs that are certain to become treasured pieces for generations to come.

Each project is shown in both a full-color photograph and a superb watercolor drawing. Such drawings have become a trademark of books written and illustrated by Margaret Boyles. Full-size patterns and easy-to-follow directions make stitching these tiny treasures pure pleasure.

We hope you'll find stitching these little beauties a rewarding endeavor. Your creations are sure to become tomorrow's heirlooms.

Mary Williams, Editor

MEREDITH® PRESS
An Imprint of Meredith® Books

MINIATURE QUILTS
Editor: Mary Williams
Designer: Tom Wegner
Technical Editor: Cheri Tamm Raymond
Copy Editor: Sydne Matus
Photography: Margaret Boyles, Liz Lyon
Cover Photography: Mike Dieter
Illustrations: Margaret Boyles
Electronic Production Coordinator: Paula Forest
Production Manager: Douglas Johnston

Vice President and Editorial Director: Elizabeth P. Rice
Executive Editor: Maryanne Bannon
Art Director: Ernest Shelton
Managing Editor: Christopher Cavanaugh

President, Book Group: Joseph J. Ward
Vice President, Retail Marketing: Jamie L. Martin
Vice President, Direct Marketing: Timothy Jarrell

On the cover: Summer Sails (page 98) and Festival Miniature (page 122)

Meredith Corporation
Chairman of the Executive Committee: E.T. Meredith III
Chairman of the Board and Chief Executive Officer: Jack D. Rehm
President and Chief Operating Officer: William T. Kerr

All of us at Meredith® Press welcome your comments and suggestions so that we may continue to bring you the best crafts products possible. Please address your correspondence to Customer Service Department, Meredith® Press, 150 East 52nd Street, New York, NY 10022 or call 1-800-678-2665.

If you would like to order additional copies of any of our books, call 1-800-678-2803 or check with your local bookstore.

Table of Contents

◇

A NOTE FROM THE AUTHOR 4

THE MINIATURE QUILT COLLECTION 6

Basket Weave Hanging   6
Country Manor   11
Nikki   20
Nikki's Drawstring Purse   30
Forever   35
Romance   40
Pastel Bear Paws   48
Victoria   56
Tiny Trees   66
A Winter's Night   73
Barrie's Vest   80
Quilted Kitties   87
Memories   92
Summer Sails   98
Precious Charmer   105
Blue Canton   110
Festival   116
Festival Miniature   122
Jeweled Star   125
Little Beauty   128

THE BASICS 138

Materials   138
The Basics of Miniature Quiltmaking   145
Foundation Piecing   154

SPECIAL TOUCHES 158

A Note from the Author

A miniature is a copy on a reduced scale, says *Webster's Ninth New Collegiate Dictionary*. What a perfect description of the wonderful little quilts we call miniatures! Although not the one-inch-to-one-foot scale makers of dollhouse furnishings and other enthusiasts use in their work, these are truly miniature if we use the dictionary definition. Most quilters define a miniature as a quilt composed of blocks that are reduced from the traditional twelve to fourteen inches to a diminutive two to five inches. The lovely quilt graphics and colors remain; only the size changes.

The first miniature quilt pattern I remember seeing is one my great-grandmother made for one of her babies. She reduced the size of the traditional Drunkard's Path blocks to one she thought more appropriate for a little quilt for a child's bed. The reduced size of the blocks makes the pattern seem much more intricate and she really did increase her work since it took so many more blocks to piece the quilt. With its lovely red and green coloring, hand piecing, and intricate quilting, it is truly a treasure.

As my own interest in little quilts grew, I began to notice that many of the wonderful doll quilts in museum collections had been constructed using reduced-size traditional patterns. Certainly the small scale was perfect for the little quilts, but there was also the practical idea that smaller size meant smaller pieces and that leftover fabrics could be stitched together to make tiny things of beauty. Some of these, made for very special dolls that were collectibles rather than toys, have been preserved in pristine condition. Others, which were obviously much loved and enjoyed, are tattered testaments to the love that goes into the construction of any quilt. Even the tiny quilts that were obviously made from scraps—even old, used fabrics—show that special feeling that lends them a soft beauty.

Old doll quilts are very difficult to find and very expensive, but now we find the miniature everywhere. Making miniature quilts is fun, practical, quick, and if the look of a collectible is needed, the piece can be antiqued to give the aura of age. The tiny blocks can be stitched into a bed-size quilt, made into a hanging or picture, worn as a textile art, made into a doll quilt, or worked into a Christmas stocking. New cutting and piecing methods, new fabrics, and adventurous new designs make these little quilts more fun than ever, while high standards of excellence in workmanship carried over from traditional quilting ensure that they can be tomorrow's heirlooms.

Often it seems that by the time they have stitched only part of a big quilt, most quilters have already mentally designed a dozen new ones. Only discipline keeps us from starting several at once. Now, with the miniature, we can finish quickly and begin another project while the idea is still new and exciting! If the design or colors don't measure up to our vision, the investment in time and fabric is minimal and we are spared the guilt of not finishing.

This book is full of little quilts—some are my adaptations of old patterns, some are completely new, and a few are a combination of old and new. Some are pieced traditionally, but most are stitched using a paper foundation that makes putting together tiny pieces a breeze. Since this work is adaptable to clothing, there are several children's patterns for inspiration. Two bright place mats should add pleasure to a cup of tea or a casual meal, while framed pictures brighten a wall. There is a nautical quilt for a little boy's nursery and a delicate pastel stenciled hanging that could easily be enlarged to make a dainty quilt for a baby girl's room. It would be fun to combine an assortment of the foundation patterns to make a sampler quilt. Just unite the various patterns with color and have fun!

If you have never made a quilt, you will find that this book is a complete manual for making miniatures. There are the basic cutting, stitching, construction, and finishing instructions needed to make the quilts shown. There are also embroidery, appliqué, antiquing, and personalizing ideas to guide you to completion.

Your scrap collection probably already contains more than enough fabric to make several miniature quilts. Only basic sewing supplies and a sewing machine are needed to get started, so browse through the collection of tiny quilts and then begin planning your first quilt. My best wishes for many happy hours!

Margaret Boyles

Basket Weave Hanging

◇

A BRIGHT BIT OF SUNSHINE FOR THE WALL

FINISHED SIZE: 17 x 17"

It's always surprising when a pattern so simple goes together to make an overall design that looks so much more complex. This little pattern is one of those. Sometimes called the Rail Fence, the basic foundation consists of just four stripes of color and is a very easy one with which to experiment.

Since this is an easy block to make using the foundation method, it appears in the **Foundation Piecing** instructions on page 155. There you will find the pattern for the tracing and detailed instructions for cutting the strips and putting one block together.

The colors chosen for this hanging are yellow and blue including a cobalt blue geometric print, a light blue with a paint splatter design in several shades of blue, a yellow calico with tiny blue flowers, and a solid yellow. The two colors that are placed on the outside edges of the blocks tend to dominate the pattern since they create the zigzag that runs diagonally across the quilt. For this quilt, they are the cobalt blue and solid yellow.

Materials

- ☐ Cobalt blue geometric cotton print: ¼ yard
- ☐ Light blue splatter cotton print: 1 fat quarter
- ☐ Yellow floral cotton print: 1 fat quarter
- ☐ Solid yellow cotton: ¾ yard
- ☐ Heirloom-weight batting: 19x19"
- ☐ Transparent nylon quilting thread
- ☐ 60-weight cotton mercerized thread: yellow
- ☐ 60-weight cotton mercerized thread: off-white for piecing

Cutting Guide

This is the kind of design in which it is easier and faster to cut long strips of the block fabric and snip off the right length as you stitch.

Cut strips for the 36 blocks as follows:
- ☐ **Cobalt blue geometric print: 1⅛" wide and 1" wide.**
- ☐ **Yellow solid: 1⅛" wide and 1" wide**
- ☐ **Light blue splatter print: 1" wide**
- ☐ **Yellow floral print: 1" wide**

In addition to the strips to make the 36 blocks, cut:
- ☐ **From the cobalt blue geometric print:**
    - **2 strips 1 x 12" for the inside border**
    - **2 strips 1 x 13¼" for the inside border**
    - **2 strips 1½ x 17" for the binding**
    - **2 strips 1½ x 18" for the binding**
- ☐ **From the yellow solid: 1 square 19 x 19" for the backing**

CENTER PANEL

Make 36 copies of the **Foundation Pattern for Basket Weave** on page 156. Following the instructions for making a block beginning on page 155 and using off-white sewing thread and a 1.5-mm stitch length, cut and piece 36 squares. Make all the blocks alike. Place the colors on the blocks as shown by the blocks in **Figure 1**. Cut the strips long enough to reach to the cutting line on the foundation. Use the 1⅛"-wide yellow and cobalt blue strips at the

(continued)

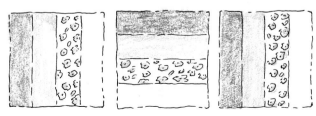

Figure 1

(continued)

outside edges so those pieces will also extend to the cutting line.

Lay the squares out in 6 rows of 6 blocks each, alternating one horizontal block with one vertical, following the color drawing of the quilt to place them in the Basket Weave pattern. Notice on the drawing of the quilt that when the blocks are placed vertically, the cobalt blue is always on the left. When the block is horizontal, the cobalt blue is always at the top.

Stitch together the 6 blocks laid out as a horizontal row. Use the neatly trimmed blocks and align the stitching lines on the paper to make perfect seams. Repeat for the 5 remaining rows.

Join the 6 strips of blocks to make the square center panel. Press the piece, but do not remove the paper.

BORDERS

With the right sides together, stitch the two 12" cobalt blue inside border pieces to the sides of the center panel with a ¼" seam. Trim the seam to ⅛" and press well. Although there is no paper in the border strips, they will stitch to the paper accurately.

Stitch the two 13¼" cobalt blue strips to the other sides. Trim and press.

Border Blocks Cutting Guide

- ☐ **Cut 72 solid yellow pieces** 2½ x ¾"
- ☐ **Cut 12 cobalt blue pieces** 2½ x 1"
- ☐ **Cut 12 cobalt blue pieces** 2 x ¾"
- ☐ **Cut 4 solid yellow pieces** 2 x ¾"
- ☐ **Cut 12 solid yellow pieces** 1¾ x ¾"
- ☐ **Cut 12 light blue pieces** 1¾ x ¾"
- ☐ **Cut 4 light blue pieces 1 x 1"**
- ☐ **Cut 8 light blue pieces 2 x 1"**
- ☐ **Cut 8 solid yellow pieces** 1¾ x ¾"
- ☐ **Cut 12 yellow print pieces** 1 x 1"
- ☐ **Cut 8 solid yellow pieces** 1 x 1"

Assembling the Border Blocks

Again, you may prefer to work in a less organized, but just as efficient manner, cutting ¾" wide strips of each color and simply snipping off the needed lengths as you sew.

Using solid yellow and the **Foundation Pattern for Yellow Border Piece** on page 10, make 8 solid yellow sections.

Using the **Foundation Pattern for Corner Block** on page 10, make 4 blocks, placing the colors as shown in **Figure 2**. Make all 4 exactly alike.

Figure 2

Again using the **Foundation Pattern for Corner Block,** make 8 blocks, assorting and arranging the colors as shown in **Figure 3**. Make 4 blocks alike, then turn the paper pattern over and stitch on the other side to make 4 blocks that are a mirror image of the first four.

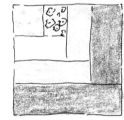

Figure 3

Assembling the Border

Stitch a pair of the **Figure 3** mirror-image blocks together so the two blue sides are in the seam. Repeat three more times.

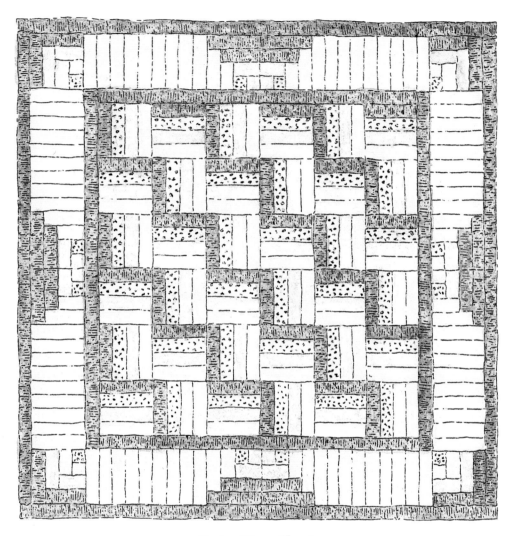

Basket Weave Hanging

Stitch a long yellow border piece to each side of the joined pairs.

Noting that the cobalt blue stripes are on the outside edge, join 2 of the strips to the sides of the piece. Press the seams and trim.

Stitch a corner block to each end of the remaining 2 border pieces. Place them all alike so the cobalt blue corners are on the outside of the border. Use the color drawing of the quilt as a guide.

Join these 2 border pieces to the top and bottom of the piece. Press and trim the seams.

(continued)

9

(continued)

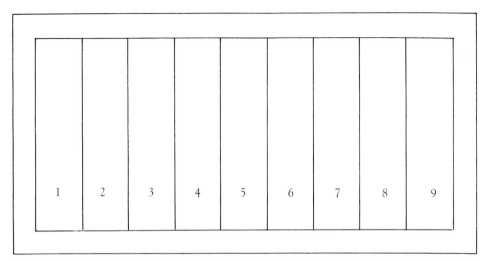

Foundation Pattern for Yellow Border Piece

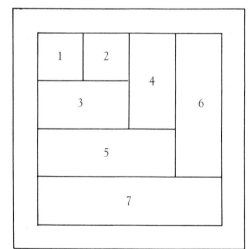

Foundation Pattern for Corner Block

QUILTING

Remove the paper foundation pieces. Press.

Layer the pieced top, the batting, and the backing, smoothing out any wrinkles. Center the top so the batting and backing extend an equal amount on all four sides.

Pin or baste the layers together.

Using transparent nylon thread on top and yellow thread in the bobbin, quilt the design by stitching "in the ditch" on all seams. Use a 3-mm length stitch. Pull all thread ends through to the back, knot them, thread the ends into a needle, and bury them in the batting.

FINISHING

Carefully trim the batting and backing so they extend ¼" beyond the quilt top on all four sides.

Stitch the 2 cobalt blue 17" binding strips to the side edges. Place the raw edge of the binding along the raw edge of the quilt top and stitch in a ¼" seam. Press the seam. Fold the binding to back of the quilt and slip-stitch to the backing to just cover machine stitching line, thus creating a ½" blue border on the right side.

Stitch the two longer binding strips to the remaining unfinished edges. Turn them back and finish to match the first two.

Country Manor

GARDEN TREASURE FOR THE BREAKFAST TABLE

FINISHED SIZE: 12 x 18"

The stylized rose design—often called the Mosaic Rose—that forms the corners of this place mat is part of a family of designs that are traditionally pieced using the foundation method. Reduced so that the block is just 3½", and made as this one was from five closely related

(continued)

shades of rose surrounded by deep green "leaves," the rose is even prettier in miniature than it is full size. Appliquéd vines connecting the roses are a pretty finishing touch. Quilting adds beauty and insulation to this bright addition to the breakfast table.

Beginning with the palest of five shades of rose as the tiny center block and working outward with the four successive shades gives the mosaic-like rose a delicate shading, which is further enhanced when the quilting has been stitched. The colors used in this piece were purchased off the bolt in a nearby quilt shop, but many quilters are beginning to experiment with custom-dyeing fabric to obtain graduations of color like this. If you have some of this hand-dyed fabric and have wondered what to do with it, the rose could be the answer.

If you have never tried the foundation piecing method, the basics are covered for you on page 154.

Rose Place Mat

One place mat can be cut from a 13½" piece of cotton providing both edges have been torn or cut with a rotary cutter to be certain they are straight. The 15" measurement in the materials list allows for this straightening.

Materials for One Place Mat

- ☐ **White cotton muslin, 42" wide: 15"**
- ☐ **Dark green cotton print: 1 fat quarter**
- ☐ **Five shades of pink cotton, #1 being the lightest, #5 the deepest:**
  Pink #1: 2 x 2"
  Pink #2: 4 x 4"
  Pink #3: 6 x 6"
  Pink #4: 6 x 6"
  Pink #5: 8 x 6"
- ☐ **Heirloom-weight batting: 13½ x 19"**
- ☐ **80-weight cotton mercerized thread: white and dark green or black**
- ☐ **60-weight cotton mercerized thread: white for quilting and construction**

To be sure that one complete mat is cut from a 13½" piece, cut as follows:

Begin by straightening one end of the white cotton, if necessary. Measure down the selvage edge and make a cut 13½" from the top. Tear or cut across the full width of the fabric. Measure 19" across the cut edge and cut at that point to make the place mat backing 13½ x19".

Cutting Guide

- ☐ **From the white cotton cut:**
  1 piece 13½ x 19"
  2 pieces 11½ x 4"
  1 piece 11½ x 5½"
  2 pieces 5½ x 4"
- ☐ **From the dark green cut enough 1"-wide bias strips to total 65"**
- ☐ **In addition, cut the small pieces for the rose listed in *Making a Block* (page 13)**

Measure across the cut edge 11½" and cut a piece that will be 11½ x 13½". Cut this into 3 pieces— one 11½ x 5½", two 11½ x 4".

Cut the two 5½ x 4" pieces from the balance of the fabric.

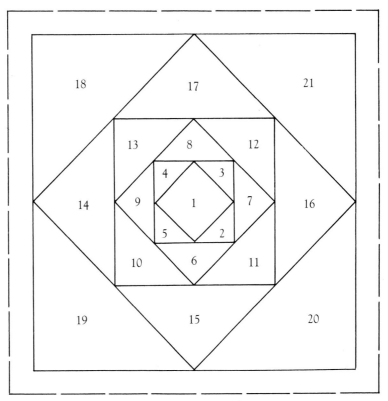

Foundation Pattern for 3½" Block

Cutting Guide for One 3½" Block

- ☐ **For the center: a square of pink #1, 1 x 1"**
- ☐ **For pieces 2, 3, 4, and 5: rectangles of pink #2, 1 x ⅝"**
- ☐ **For pieces 6, 7, 8, and 9: rectangles of pink #3, 1⅜ x ¾"**
- ☐ **For pieces 10, 11, 12, and 13: rectangles of pink #4, 1½ x 1"**
- ☐ **For pieces 14, 15, 16, and 17: rectangles of pink #5, 2 x 1½"**
- ☐ **For the corner triangles cut 2 dark green squares 3 x 3". Cut these in half diagonally to make the 4 leaf triangles**

MAKING A BLOCK

Trace the **Foundation Pattern for 3½" Block** and reproduce it so you have 4 block patterns on tracing paper.

Beginning with the center square of pink #1 and following the numbered sequence, stitch the pieces to the tracing paper. Use the colors in sequence from the lightest to the darkest.

The final 4 triangles should be the dark green. Trim the outside edges along the cutting line.

Make 4 roses.

(continued)

(continued)

Appliqué

Marking

Trace the **Vine and Leaf Appliqué Design**, joining the two sections at the long slashed lines.

With a wash-out pen, trace the design onto the two 11½ x 4" pieces, using the edge marks to center it.

Trace only the part of the design specified for the side sections onto the two 5½ x 4" pieces. To make a mirror image of the vine curve, turn the tracing over to trace the second side.

Stitching

Following the instructions on page 168, make bias tubing for the vines. Make two pieces about 14" long and two pieces about 7" long. Press the tubing so the seam runs down the center of the pieces.

Pin the tubing to the background along the vine line with the seam down and stitch it in place. Repeat for all four sections.

(continued)

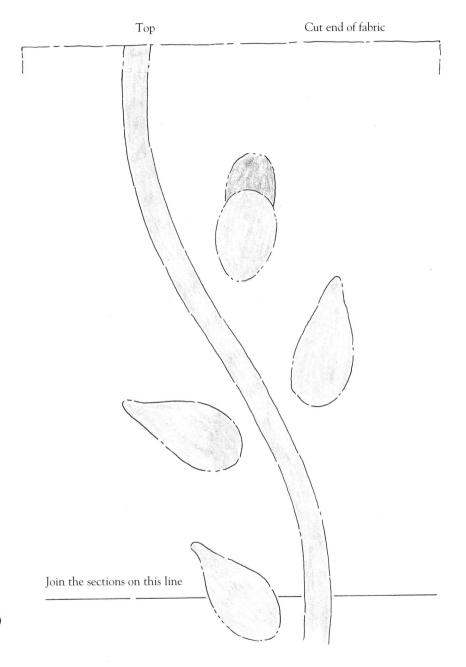

Top   Cut end of fabric

Join the sections on this line

Vine and Leaf Appliqué Design, Upper Section

(continued)

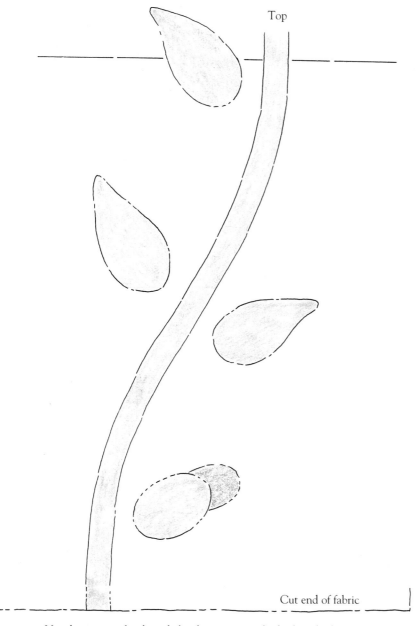

Top

Cut end of fabric

Use this section for the side borders omitting the leaf on the line.

Vine and Leaf Appliqué Design, Lower Section

Trace leaf and bud pieces. Cut these out and trace around them to mark the necessary number of leaves and buds. Use pink #3 for the tips of the buds.

Stay-stitch around the leaves and bud sheaths with the dark green or black thread. Use white thread for the pink buds.

Appliqué all the leaves and buds in place. As for the stay-stitching, use the green or black thread for all the dark green appliqués and white for the pink buds.

Rinse out any remaining markings. Iron the pieces dry, finishing on the wrong side to maintain the depth of the appliqué.

Lay out the pieces in stitching order

Figure 1

CONSTRUCTION

Lay out the 9 pieces of the place mat top as shown in **Figure 1**.

Using the 60-weight white thread, join the pieces in ¼" seams to make 3 horizontal strips. As it is sewn, press each seam and trim it to ⅛".

Join the 3 rows, carefully matching the seam lines.

Remove the paper foundations from the rose blocks.

QUILTING AND BINDING

Layer the place mat back, the batting, and the pieced top. Pin the layers together carefully.

If you quilt by hand, baste the layers together and use the white 60-weight thread for the stitching. For machine quilting, thread the machine with clear nylon thread on top and the 60-weight cotton in the bobbin and work with only the pins for stabilization. Use the lines on the color drawing of the place mat as a guide for placement of the quilting lines.

Quilt "in the ditch" on all seam lines joining the pieces together.

Outline-quilt along the edges of the appliqués.

Quilt ¼" inside the seams of the five white areas.

Quilt "in the ditch" on all seam lines of the roses.

Seam the dark green bias strips to make one continuous piece 65" long.

Trim the outside edges of the place mat so all layers are even and the edges straight.

With right sides together and matching the raw edges, stitch the bias strip to the right side of the place mat in a ¼" seam. Allow ease at the corners. Turn the bias to the wrong side and hem it to the place mat. *(continued)*

(continued)

Rose Napkin

The pictured napkin is one that was purchased ready-made. It is a 16" square of heavy cotton trimmed with one-inch wide crocheted cotton lace. A similar napkin can easily be made from cotton or linen finished with a narrow hem and attached heavy lace.

Begin by making the tiny—this is really a miniature—rose block. The

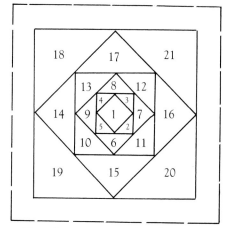

Foundation Pattern for 1¾" Block

Materials for One Napkin

- ☐ 1 white cotton napkin: 16x16"
- ☐ Very small scraps of the colors used for the roses on the place mat
- ☐ For machine embroidery, 50-weight cotton mercerized thread: dark green
- ☐ For hand embroidery, 6-strand cotton embroidery floss: 2 yards dark green

pieces are small, but since you have already made the four larger blocks, the procedure is familiar and the piece goes together surprisingly well.

Make the block exactly like the larger ones in terms of the colors. Trace the *Foundation Pattern for 1¾" Block* to make a tracing paper backing for the rose.

You will find that if you cut the little pieces a bit larger than needed and trim them after each has been stitched, they are easier to work with.

After the final green triangles have been stitched, add a straight strip of pink about ¼" wide to each of the four edges. Stitch these on the seam line and let them extend beyond the block edges.

Place the napkin on corner of the *Embroidery Design for the Rose Napkin* (page 19) drawing and mark the position of the block and embroidery design.

Using dark green thread, embroider the vines and leaves either by machine or by hand. For machine embroidery use the dark green cotton thread and embroider the vine with a 4-mm satin stitch. To make a leaf, use one of your machine embroidery patterns or shape satin stitches to form one.

For hand embroidery use 3 strands of cotton embroidery floss to work the vines in chain stitch and the leaves in fishbone stitch.

Turn the pink edge of the pieced block to the back so just a tiny rim of color shows. Appliqué the block in place.

Embroidery Design for the Rose Napkin

Nikki

◇

The pinafore bib—a large collar that ties at the underarms—is a versatile accessory for a little girl. The little bit of extra length lends the collar importance, while the ribbon ties hold it in place and add an extra flourish. The bib can be very tailored, embroidered, quilted like this one, or lavished with lace and ribbons. All look sweet and can change the mood of a dress completely.

Materials

- ☐ **White batiste or fine quilter's cotton, 42" wide: 12"**
- ☐ **Batiste or quilter's muslin for bib lining, 42" wide: 23 x 28"**
- ☐ **The dress fabric, 42" wide: about ⅛ yard**
- ☐ **Rose cotton and green cotton: 6 x 6" of each**
- ☐ **Lightweight fleece made for quilted clothing: 23 x 28"**
- ☐ **60-weight cotton mercerized thread for construction**
- ☐ **50-weight cotton mercerized thread: white for quilting**
- ☐ **50-weight cotton mercerized thread: black for quilting**
- ☐ **Six-strand cotton embroidery floss for button loops: several yards of white**
- ☐ **1¼"-wide double-faced satin ribbon: 2½ to 3 yards depending on the size of the bib**
- ☐ **Small-shank back buttons: 4**

The Dress Worn with a Pinafore Bib

The bib will fit comfortably over many dresses, but is most successful with a relatively simple dress constructed with an Empire waist. This is a raised waistline in which the yoke extends about 2" below the armhole like the one in the drawing on page 24. If you wish to make a new dress for your little one, look in the pattern books for a classic dress like this. The dress can be finished with a Peter Pan collar, which is then worn outside the bib for an extra touch of prettiness.

(continued)

Cutting Guide

- ☐ **From the bib fabric, cut the bib front and 2 backs**
- ☐ **From the dark print dress fabric, cut 1"-wide strips of fabric noted by dashed lines on the pattern pieces**
- ☐ **From the dark print, cut enough 1"-wide bias strips to total 75"**

If you can't find a pattern with an Empire yoke, choose a basic dress with a bodice fitted to the waist.

Then cut off the bodice as shown in **Figure 1** to make the Empire yoke. Measure down the side seam below the armhole 2½" to 3" depending on the size, and cut off the bodice pattern. This allows for two ½" seams—one for the sleeve, the other to attach the yoke to the skirt. If the pattern has a curved bottom edge like the one shown in the drawing, maintain that curve. Add to the length of the skirt the measurement of the cut-away portion of the bodice.

Cut the bodice of dress pattern to make an Empire Yoke

Figure 1

The dress shown with the bib (at left) was made from a black-background cotton brightened with small sprays of rose and pink flowers. The print was ideal for use with the picture foundation block, since individual flowers could be framed in the quilted blocks. The dotted Swiss collar and sleeves make the dress one that is just as pretty without the bib. Ribbon ties to match the flowers trim the sleeves and tie the bib at the underarm.

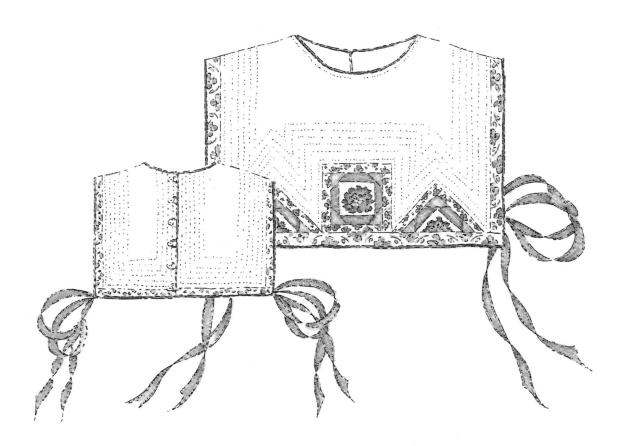

Lightweight batiste for the bib and the use of quilting fleece as batting keep the bulk of the bib to a minimum. Either imported cotton batiste or a blend of polyester and cotton batiste will be good in this pattern.

MAKING THE BORDER BLOCKS

Trace the **Foundation Pattern for Center Block** once. Trace the **Foundation Pattern for Triangular Blocks** twice.

Decide which portion of the pattern in the dress fabric should be the center square and the triangles. Cut those 3 pieces large enough to allow ¼" seam allowances. Cut strips of the rose, the green, and the dress print for the other pieces.

Placing the colors where shown on the foundation patterns, and working in the numbered stitching order, construct the 3 blocks. Trim them even with the cutting lines on the paper. Press.

Remove the paper foundations.

(continued)

◇

(continued)

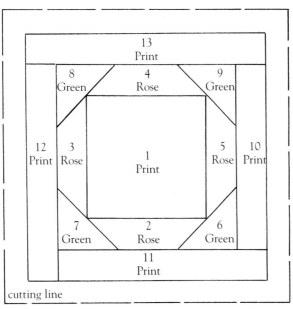

13
Print

8
Green

4
Rose

9
Green

12
Print

3
Rose

1
Print

5
Rose

10
Print

7
Green

2
Rose

6
Green

11
Print

cutting line

Foundation Pattern for Center Block

The Empire yoke dress looks best with the bibs

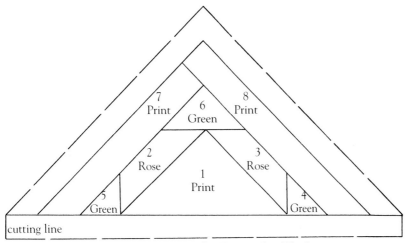

7
Print

6
Green

8
Print

2
Rose

3
Rose

1
Print

5
Green

4
Green

cutting line

Foundation Pattern for Triangular Blocks

Neatly turn the ¼" seam allowances to the wrong side on the two sides of the triangles. Repeat for the top and two sides of the square.

CONSTRUCTION

Trace the **Pinafore Bib Pattern** pieces (pages 25, 27, 28, and 29) for the size you are making. Join the pieces at the slashed line to make full-size pattern pieces. Note the slashed lines that are ¾" from the side and bottom edges of the size 3 pattern. For the other sizes, trace the slashed line at the bottom of the pattern. Then measure in ¾" from

(continued)

24

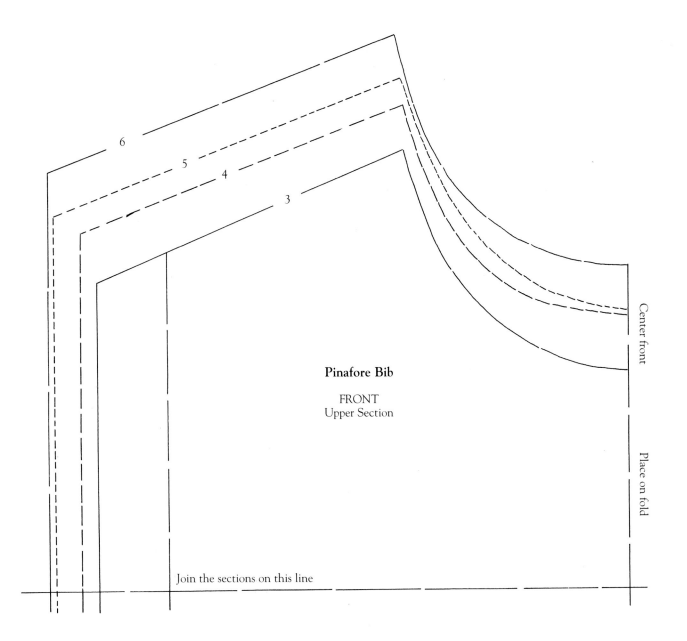

6

5

4

3

Pinafore Bib

FRONT
Upper Section

Center front

Place on fold

Join the sections on this line

the side edges and place the lines on your pattern piece.

With right sides together, place a strip of border fabric on the slashed line with the raw edge ¼" across the line as shown by **Figure 2**. Stitch on the line. Stitch the four pieces to the sides first, extending them all the way to the ends. Trim the seams to ⅛" and press the dark border flat.

Stitch the print strips to the lower edges of the back sections, placing them as for the sides. Let the pieces extend all the way to the edges of

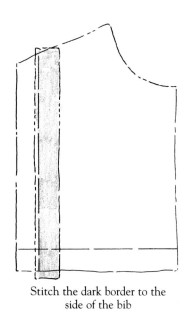

Stitch the dark border to the side of the bib

Figure 2

the sections. Trim the seams and press. The backs look like **Figure 3**.

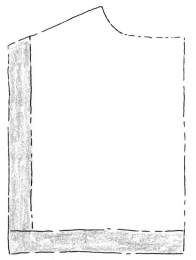

One side of the bib back with the borders sewn and pressed

Figure 3

Place the completed border blocks on the bib front with the raw edges extending across the dashed line as shown on the pattern piece. Place the three pieces so they just touch each other at the line as on the pattern piece. The unpressed raw edge extends ¼" below the line. On larger sizes there will be a wider space between the end of the triangle and the border at the outside edge.

Place the front border strip over the pinned blocks, right sides together and raw edges matching. Pin the strip. Stitch in a ¼" seam. Trim the seam to ⅛" and press the border flat.

Pin the border blocks flat. Using dark thread and the appliqué whip-stitch, stitch the tops of the blocks to the batiste.

Stitch the front to the backs at the shoulders making a ⅜" seam. Press the seam open.

Following the instructions on page 153, make enough piping to reach around the entire bib, including the neck edge (about 75").

Trim the piping to a ¼" width. Beginning at the back neck on the left side and matching the raw edges, stitch the piping to the entire perimeter of the bib—including the neck edge—making a ¼" seam.

QUILTING

Spread out the bib lining rectangle with the fleece rectangle on top. Smooth out any wrinkles.

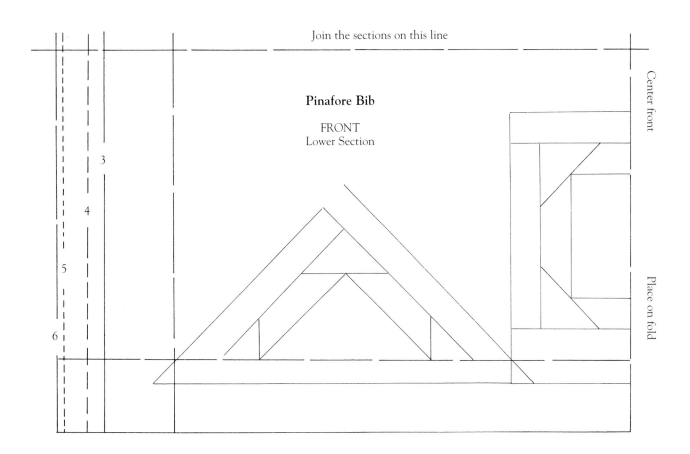

Join the sections on this line

Pinafore Bib

FRONT
Lower Section

Center front

Place on fold

3

4

5

6

Place the bib right side up on top of the fleece. Pin the layers together. Baste, placing the rows about 2" apart.

Use the 50-weight white cotton thread for quilting in the white areas. Use the black thread in the blocks and front border.

Placing the stitches close to the seam, quilt along the edge of the black border following the outline of the blocks on the front.

Trim the surplus fleece and backing on the outside edges of the bib leaving a ¼" seam allowance. Trim away an extra ¼" of the fleece to eliminate bulk in the seam.

Turn the raw edges to the inside and whipstitch them together to finish the outside edge.

With white thread, place a row of quilting stitches ¼" from the black border. Begin the first row at the neck edge at the back and work all

(continued)

(continued)

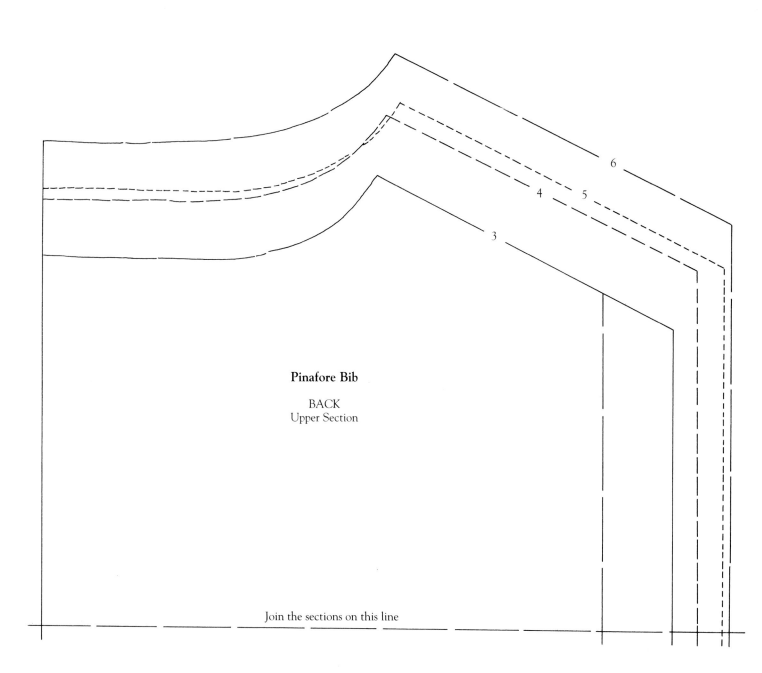

6

4   5

3

Pinafore Bib

BACK
Upper Section

Join the sections on this line

Pinafore Bib

BACK
Lower Section

3

4

5

6

Join the sections on this line

the way around the bib following the shapes of the appliqué patches on the front.

Following the quilting line already established, place 5 more rows of stitching all ¼" apart. Use the color drawing of the bib as a guide for quilting.

FINISHING

Using 2 strands of embroidery floss, make a ½"-long buttonhole loop at each of the four corners of the bib at the underarms. Place these on the wrong side about ¼" from the edges.

Mark the left back for placement of the buttons and sew them about ¼" from the edge.

Make small buttonhole loops on the right side of the back.

Cut the ribbon into 2 equal pieces. Thread one end through a loop on the front and through the corresponding loop on the back. Tie pretty bows.

Nikki's Drawstring Purse

A PLACE FOR TINY TREASURES

FINISHED SIZE: APPROXIMATELY 8 x 5"

*E*very little girl loves a purse and finds countless little things to tuck away in it. When it matches a special dress, it is doubly delightful. This is a very easy pattern that lets you use some of the miniature quilt blocks in a novel way. Minimal quilting makes this a fast project.

Materials

- ☐ Black quilter's cotton, 42" wide: ¼ yard
- ☐ Dark print cotton: a quilter's quarter
- ☐ Rose cotton and green cotton: 6x6" of each
- ☐ Heavy interfacing: 8x4"
- ☐ Quilter's fleece: 9x17"
- ☐ Fine cotton cord for piping: 1 yard
- ☐ Black satin rat-tail cord: 2 yards
- ☐ Cotton mercerized thread: black

Cutting Guide

- ☐ From the black cotton, cut 2 rectangles 9x17" and 2 oval purse bottoms
- ☐ From the interfacing, cut 1 purse bottom
- ☐ From the dark print, cut a strip 1x17" and enough 1"-wide bias strips to total 1 yard

---

CONSTRUCTION

Following the instructions for making the border blocks for the **Pinafore Bib** (page 23), construct 2 square blocks and 4 triangular blocks.

Remove the paper from the blocks and press back the ¼" seam allowance on the sides (but not the bases) of the triangles and all four sides of the square blocks.

Place the triangular blocks along one long edge of the purse fabric rectangle with the raw edges matching, evenly spaced along edges as shown in **Figure 1** (page 32). There should be about ¼" between the ends of the triangles. Allow ½" for the side seam as also shown in Figure 1. Pin them in place.

With right sides together, pin the print border strip over the triangles and stitch them in a ¼" seam. Press the seam toward the border.

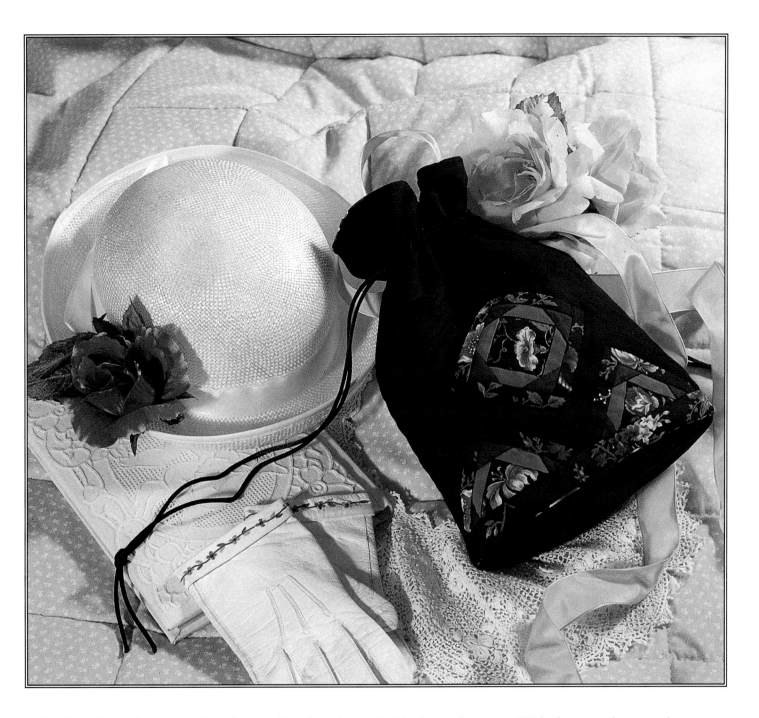

Hand-appliqué the loose sides of the triangles to the purse fabric.

Turn the 2 square blocks on point with ½" between the edges of the two sets of blocks as shown in **Figure 1.**

Hand-appliqué the blocks to the purse fabric.

Following the instructions on page 153, make 36" of corded piping. Trim the seam allowance on the piping to an even ¼".

With the raw edges matching, stitch part of the piping to the border print in a ¼" seam.

Stitch the remaining piece of piping to the top edge of the purse, also making a ¼" seam.

(continued)

◇

(continued)

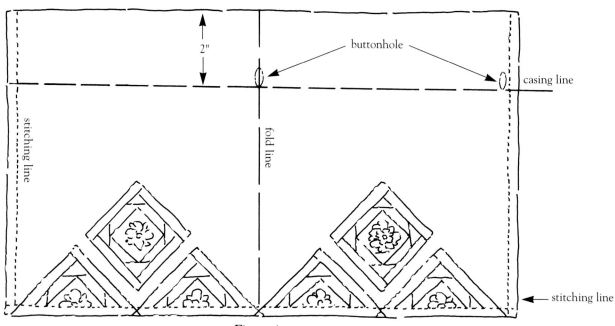

Figure 1

Measure down from the top edge 2" and draw a line for a casing stitching row as shown in **Figure 1.**

QUILTING

Pin the fleece to the wrong side of the appliquéd rectangle. Baste.

Using black thread, quilt by hand or machine. Outline-quilt around each block or triangle. Quilt "in the ditch" along the seam line of the print border. Then following the shapes of the blocks, quilt in a chevron pattern as shown in the color drawing. Place the rows a generous ¼" apart. Six rows of this echo quilting should reach almost to the stitching line for the casing.

Quilt "in the ditch" on all the seam lines of the pieced blocks.

FINISHING

Making a ½" seam and with right sides together, stitch the short sides of the rectangle together.

Pin the interfacing to the wrong side of the purse bottom piece. Stitch them together, placing the row of stitching about ¼" from the edge.

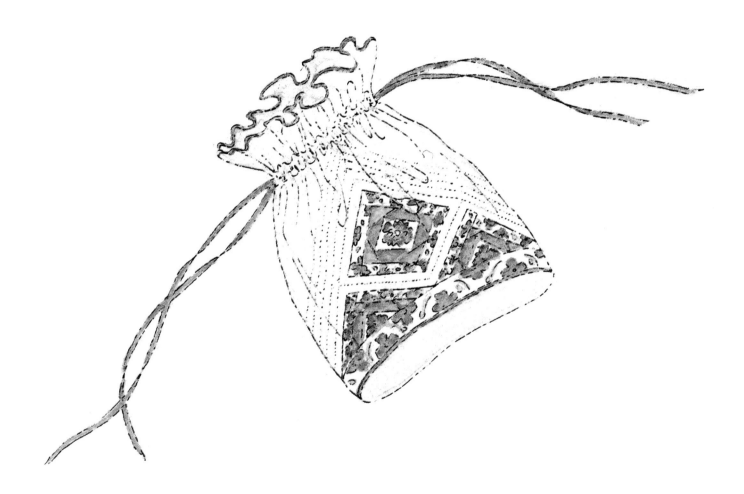

Pin the bottom to the purse tube. Stitch in a ¼" seam.

Make a ½"-long vertical buttonhole beside the seam, placing it so the bottom is on the line for the casing as shown in **Figure 1.**

Make another buttonhole on the opposite side, placing it on the fold line as noted in **Figure 1.**

Stitch the side seam of the lining and attach the bottom piece as for the purse.

(continued)

(continued)

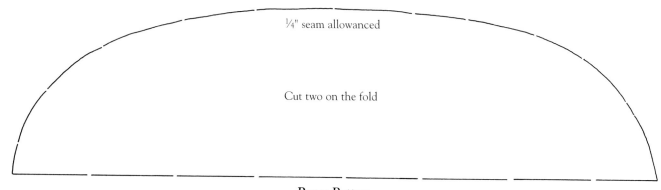

¼" seam allowanced

Cut two on the fold

Purse Bottom

Slip the lining into the purse, matching the side seams. Pin along the top edge.

Turn the raw edges to the inside and whipstitch along the piping to finish the top edge.

Stitch on the casing line and again ½" above it to make a tube for the drawstrings.

Cut the rat-tail cord in half to make 2 pieces. Attach a safety pin to one end and thread one piece through the casing. Go all the way around the purse, beginning and ending in the same buttonhole.

Begin and end the other strand in the opposite buttonhole.

Tie the ends together. Pull the drawstrings to close the top of the purse.

Forever

◇

A QUILTED WEDDING TREASURE

FINISHED SIZE: 7 x 7" PLUS 3½" LACE RUFFLE

(continued)

*T*he ring bearer, carefully carrying his lace-trimmed white satin pillow with rings glistening in the candlelight of the church, always makes his journey down the aisle to the accompaniment of a soft adoring hum. Who could resist such a little angel?

The pillow he carries is usually a confection of laces and satin, a fitting resting place for the precious rings. This little pieced and quilted version of the traditional pillow is one that any bride would treasure and long keep as part of her wedding mementos. For a quilter, it is a chance to indulge in stitching with satin ribbon to make an unusual and beautiful accessory for the wedding.

Made from white satin ribbons and stitched by the foundation piecing method, the little pillow is constructed from four 2½" blocks devised from part of a Log Cabin block. Rose jacquard and crinkly, textured ribbon borders edge the square. A bow of the textured ribbon, a wide ruffle of beautiful lace, and a double layer of tulle add the final flourishes.

Materials

- ☐ White satin ribbon, ⅝" wide: 1 yard
- ☐ White satin ribbon, ¾" wide: ½ yard
- ☐ White satin ribbon with white rose jacquard pattern, ⅝" wide: 1 yard
- ☐ White satin ribbon with white rose jacquard pattern, 1⅜" wide: 1 yard
- ☐ White crinkled satin ribbon, 1" wide: 3 yards
- ☐ Heirloom-weight batting: 8x8"
- ☐ White batiste for lining: 8x16"
- ☐ White bridal satin or faille: 9x9"
- ☐ White bridal tulle, 42" wide: ½ yard
- ☐ White bridal lace edging, 3" wide: 2¼ yards
- ☐ Enough loose fiberfill for a 7" pillow
- ☐ 60-weight cotton mercerized sewing thread: white
- ☐ Transparent nylon sewing thread

Cutting Guide

- ☐ **From the white batiste, cut 2 squares 8x8"**
- ☐ **From the tulle, cut 2 strips 8" wide across the width of the fabric**

Like most ring bearers' pillows, this one is small. If you wish to make yours a bit larger, buy an extra yard of the crinkled ribbon and add one more row to your squares.

MAKING THE BLOCKS

Trace the **Foundation Pattern** (page 38) and reproduce it so you have 4 copies.

It is not necessary to measure and cut the ribbons into pieces. Simply snip off pieces of the length needed as you move through the stitching order. When trimming seam allowances, leave a bit more than when you are sewing cotton to accommodate the slippery, fraying tendencies of many ribbons.

Beginning with a square of the 1" crinkled ribbon, stitch the ribbon to the foundation in the numbered order.

(continued)

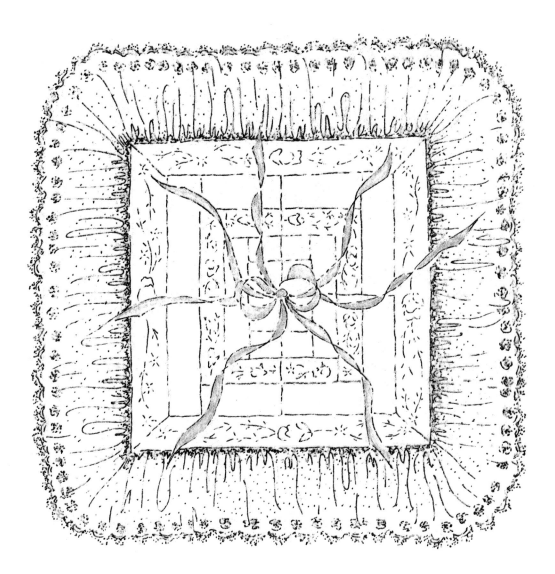

(continued)

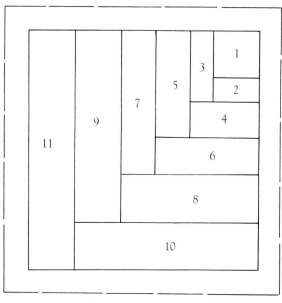

Foundation Pattern

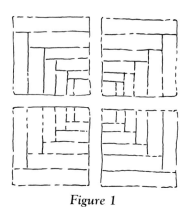

Figure 1

Square 1 is the crinkled ribbon. For 2, 3, 4, and 5, use the ⅝" white ribbon. For 6 and 7, use the ¾" white ribbon. For strips 8 and 9, use the narrow rose jacquard ribbon. Finish with the crinkled ribbon for pieces 10 and 11. Seam allowances will vary because of the ribbon widths. This is not a problem as long as each is secure.

Make 2 blocks, then turn the remaining 2 paper copies over and work from the other side to make 2 blocks that are mirror images of the first two.

CONSTRUCTION

Lay the 4 blocks in position shown in *Figure 1*.

Join the four into a square, using ¼" seam allowances. Trim the seam allowances.

Cut the yard of wide rose jacquard ribbon into four 9" pieces.

Allowing the extra length to extend equally at both ends, stitch these ribbon pieces to the sides of the square, beginning and ending the stitching ¼" from the ends of the sides.

Press the ribbon ends to form a miter. Stitch the miter.

The completed square measures 7 x 7", but since the ribbon border is the edge, it has very little seam allowance. To remedy this, cut the batiste into two 8" squares. Center the satin top on one square. Pin securely. Stitch just the edge of the rose border to the batiste.

QUILTING

Layer the top, the batting, and the other batiste square. Pin or baste.

Using the transparent nylon thread on top and the white cotton in the bobbin, machine-quilt "in the ditch" on all seam lines. Use a 2.5-mm length stitch and note that the back of this piece will be inside the pillow, so any backing up you do to end the thread will be hidden. Working in this manner, you can machine-quilt this piece in about fifteen minutes.

Finish the quilting by placing a row of stitching on the edge of the outside ribbon to hold the layers together.

MAKING THE PILLOW

Trim the edges of the quilted top to ½". In addition, trim the batting as close to the stitching as possible to eliminate bulk in the seam.

Seam the two tulle strips together to make one long ruffle piece.

Fold the tulle ruffle in half so it is 4" wide. Pin the raw edges together.

Place the lace edging on the tulle so the straight edge is ½" from the pinned raw edges. Pin. (The tulle should also extend ½" beyond the fancy edge of the lace.)

Using a 4-mm-long straight stitch and the white cotton thread, stitch 2 rows of gathering threads along the edge of the ruffle. Place the first row several threads inside the lace heading, the second ¼" below that.

If the tulle is longer than the lace, cut the extra away. Without catching the gathering threads, join the ends of the ruffle in a French seam.

Pull up the gathering threads so the ruffle fits the outside edge of the pillow top.

With right sides together—lace against satin—pin the ruffle to the pillow top. Add extra fullness at the corners so the ruffle will lie flat. Stitch.

With right sides together, pin the pillow back to the top. Stitch, leaving an opening for turning. Trim the seam and turn right side out.

Fill with loose fiberfill. Stitch the opening closed with invisible stitches.

With the extra crinkled ribbon make a bow for the top of the pillow. Allow the ends to be long enough to trail prettily below the pillow when it is carried.

Romance

A TINY APPLIQUÉ TREASURE

FINISHED SIZE: 10 X 11½"

This is a real quilt, appliquéd, piped, and quilted just like a full-size one, but tiny—just the right size to hang in a little girl's room or in that dark corner of the powder room that needs a touch of color. That touch comes from a collection of dainty calico prints in romantic soft pastels that look like they might be scraps of beloved dresses long since outgrown.

The bow and vines are made from bias tubing, an easy way to appliqué long curving pieces without the need to turn back hem edges. Although small, the other appliqué pieces are shaped to be easy to apply.

CENTER PANEL

Trace one of the hearts on the **Center Panel** drawing (page 42) and make a paper template, cutting exactly on the outline. Center the template on one of the 2" pastel print squares and use a wash-out pen to trace the heart. Repeat to make 6, cutting the sixth from the ¼-yard pink pastel print piece.

Using a 1.5-mm straight stitch, 80-weight cotton sewing thread, and a size 70 needle, machine-stay-stitch around the hearts, placing the stitching exactly on the outlines as shown in **Figure 1**.

Rinse out the blue outlines. Press the squares flat. Cut out the hearts leaving a ⅛" turnback for a hem beyond the stitching lines.

On the white cotton, trace the center panel rectangle and the interior dividing lines from the **Center Panel** drawing on page 42.

Materials
- [ ] White cotton: ½ yard
- [ ] Pink pastel cotton print: ¼ yard
- [ ] 5 pastel cotton prints: 2x2" of each
- [ ] Pale blue cotton print for ribbons: 1 fat quarter
- [ ] Pale green cotton print for vines and leaves: 1 fat quarter
- [ ] Pink cotton print for flowers and buds: 6x6"
- [ ] 60-weight cotton mercerized thread: white
- [ ] 80-weight cotton mercerized thread: white
- [ ] Very fine cotton cord for piping: 52"
- [ ] Heirloom-weight batting: 12x14"

Cutting Guide
- [ ] From the white cut:
  - 1 piece 7x9"
  - 2 pieces 11x13"
  - Enough 1"-wide bias strips to total 52"
- [ ] From the pale blue print for ribbons cut: enough 1"-wide bias strips to total 54"
- [ ] From the pale green print for vines cut: enough 1"-wide bias strips to total 24"
- [ ] Cut the hearts, flowers, and leaves as directed in the instructions

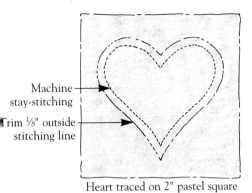

Machine stay-stitching

Trim ⅛" outside stitching line

Heart traced on 2" pastel square

Figure 1

While the heart outlines are not needed, you may wish to make several reference marks to help in centering the appliqués.

APPLIQUÉ HEARTS

Arrange the hearts so the colors are pleasing and balanced.

Pin one heart in place, centering it in the square on the white fabric as in **Figure 2** (page 42).

Baste the heart with small stitches placed a generous ⅛" inside the stitched outline as in **Figure 2.** (The basting allows the hem to be turned to the inside as you stitch the heart to the background fabric.)

(continued)

(continued)

Center Panel

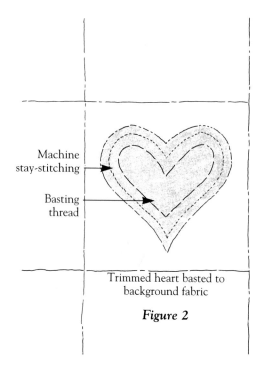

Machine stay-stitching

Basting thread

Trimmed heart basted to background fabric

Figure 2

Using tiny invisible stitches and turning the hem under as you work, stitch the hearts to the white background. As you turn the hem under, roll the stay-stitching just beyond the edge of the fold so it is concealed by the hand stitches. If turning the points of the hearts is difficult, use a bit of instant bonding fabric adhesive to hold the edges back. Stitch all six hearts to the background using the color drawing of the hanging as a guide for placing the colors.

(continued)

(continued)

BIAS TUBING LATTICE

From the ¼-yard pink print piece, cut 3 bias strips 1" wide. One should be 7" long; 2 should be 5" long.

Following the instructions for making tubing on page 168, make 3 pieces of tubing ¼" wide.

Press the tubing strips so the seam is in the middle.

Pin the pieces to the white background with the seam side down. Allow the ends of the pieces to extend across the stitching line so they will be enclosed in the seam when the inner border is added. Stitch in place.

INNER BORDER

Cut 2 pink print strips 1½ x 4" and 2 strips 1½ x 8½".

Stitch the two 4" strips to the top and bottom ends of the center panel, making a ¼" seam. Trim the seam allowance to ⅛" and press it toward the print border piece.

Stitch the two 8½" border pieces to the sides of the panel, also in a ¼" seam. Trim the seam allowance to ⅛" and press it toward the print.

Make a paper template from the *Scallop Pattern*.

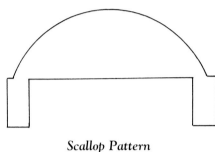

Scallop Pattern

Place the pattern on the print border with the straight edge on the seam line and the two little extensions on the bias tubing. With a wash-out pen, trace the scallop. Move the template and trace 3 scallops on each side, 2 on both the top and bottom edges.

Using the same machine setting, needle, and thread as for the hearts, stay-stitch on the scallop outline.

Trim the scallops, leaving ⅛" to turn under for a hem.

OUTSIDE BORDER

Place the scalloped panel on one of the 11 x 13" white rectangles, centering it. Pin and baste it carefully. Turn under the raw edges of the scallops and stitch them in place as for the hearts.

Cut 2 strips of pink print 1½ x 15" and 2 strips 1½ x 13". (These are a little longer than needed to allow room for alignment at the corners.)

For the top and bottom edges, fold the strips in half to find the centers, then place the scallop template as shown in **Figure 3** with the scallop edge ⅛" from the cut edge. Beginning at the center as shown, trace the scallops to the ends of the strips.

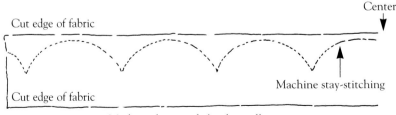

Marking the outside border scallops

Figure 3

For the sides, work as for the other two pieces, but place the widest part of the scallop at the center point so the scallops will echo those on the small panel.

Using the same machine setting, needle, and thread as used previously, stay-stitch on the scallop lines of all four border pieces. Rinse out the blue lines, iron dry, and trim the scallops as before.

Mark the centers of the white borders on the panel. Place the piece on a flat surface and lay the scalloped pink border pieces on it, matching the center points and aligning the raw edges of white and pink. The stay-stitched lines should cross to form a little scallop at the corners.

To form mitered corners of the scalloped frame, lay a right triangle at each corner and mark a diagonal stitching line from the outside corner to the edge of the scalloped piece on both pink layers. Pin the pieces together, and with right sides together, stitch a seam. Stitch all

(continued)

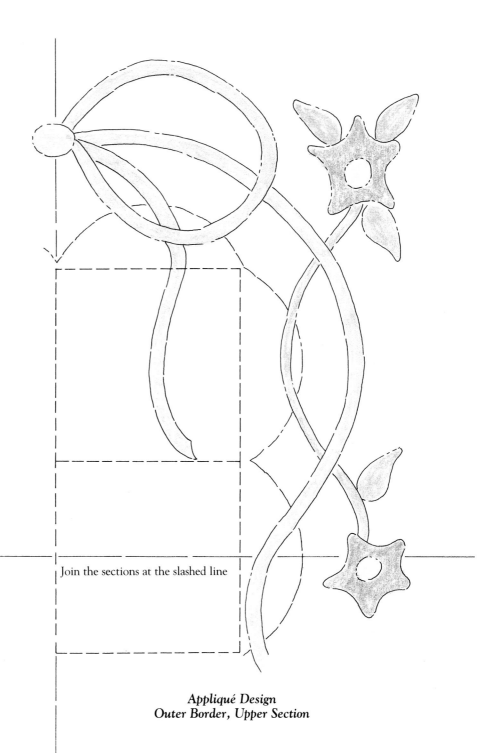

Join the sections at the slashed line

**Appliqué Design
Outer Border, Upper Section**

◇

(continued)

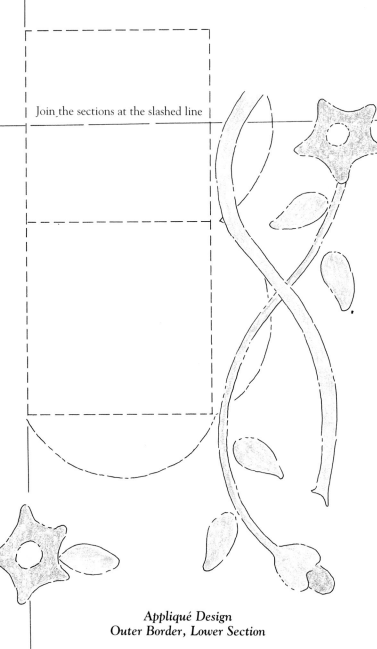

Join the sections at the slashed line

**Appliqué Design
Outer Border, Lower Section**

four corners to form a frame. Finger-press the seams open and lay the piece on the panel to check the fit before trimming the seams and pressing again.

Machine-baste the two layers together along the outside edge, placing the line of stitches ¼" from the edge.

Press. Pin and baste the scallops in place, then turn under the raw edges and stitch them to the white with invisible appliqué stitches.

Piece together the 1" white bias strips and make corded piping, following the directions on page 153.

Matching the raw edges, stitch the corded piping to the outside edge of the piece.

APPLIQUÉ

Trace the two sections of the *Appliqué Design*, joining them at the long slashed lines to make one drawing of half the outer border. The outline of the center panel and its scalloped border have been shown on the drawing in short slashed lines to help you with placement of the appliqué designs. Place the quilt over the drawing and trace the design with a wash-out pen.

Trace the flowers, leaves, and circular flower centers and cut little paper templates to trace on the color fabric indicated. These will be easier to appliqué if they are stay-stitched like the hearts.

Stitch the various appliqué pieces to the border. Beginning with the leaves, which are the lower layer, work upward to the vines, flowers, flower centers, and finally the blue ribbons.

Using bias tubing for the ribbons and vines eliminates much tedious effort to turn back edges on the slender pieces. Following the instructions on page 168, make short pieces of tubing—for example, four 6"-long pieces of green for the vines—to make turning easier. As

for the pink lattice pieces, finger-press the tubing so the seam is in the center and sew it down with the seam side down.

Both the vine and the ribbon bias strips begin as 1"-wide pieces. Stitch the blue ones $\frac{1}{4}$" from the fold and the vine pieces $\frac{1}{8}$" from the fold so the vines will be narrower than the ribbons. It is necessary to trim the seam allowances close in order to turn the strips. Leave the end wider to make beginning to turn easier.

When all the appliqué has been completed, rinse out any blue lines showing. Place a towel on the ironing board and iron the piece dry. Finish by pressing well on the wrong side to maintain the raised dimension of the appliqués.

QUILTING

Layer the quilt top, the batting, and the white backing. Smooth out any wrinkles and pin them together.

Baste and remove the pins.

Using the 60-weight white cotton thread, quilt around each appliqué motif, the scalloped borders, and the hearts.

In addition, quilt $\frac{1}{4}$" inside the scalloped borders.

FINISHING

Trim the three layers even. Then cut an additional $\frac{1}{4}$" from the batting.

Turn the raw edges to the inside and whipstitch the edges together, working from the back.

Pastel Bear Paws

⬦

A LITTLE RUFFLED PILLOW

FINISHED SIZE: 10 x 10" PLUS 3" RUFFLE

Called Bear Paw in Pennsylvania and Ohio in the middle nineteenth century, this pattern was known as Duck's Foot in the Mud in New York and Hand of Friendship in Quaker Philadelphia. Each is a delightfully adept description of the design, which is usually interpreted in a 12" block. For miniature makers, the pattern is an easy one to reduce to 3½" while still retaining its interesting graphic texture

A block that is stunning in its geometric proportions when sewn in brightly contrasting colors, it is also one that changes gracefully into a softly pleasing arrangement of color when made up in blending pastels. To make a little ruffled pillow that would delight any lover of things Victorian, four of the miniature blocks stitched up in palest pink are delightful. Although it takes many little pieces to make a block, this design is an easy one to stitch in miniature. Machine quilting "in the ditch" finishes the pillow quickly.

The prints used for the pillow are five tiny calicos and a delicate plaid. For the lightest, a white-on-white floral was chosen. The medium pink prints used for the paw pads are three florals and a sweet bow pattern. A fine-line plaid in medium pink works beautifully as block centers, lattice strips, and borders.

The pillow back is cut from the pink plaid; the tiny piping and the wider ruffle are the white-on-white print. Fine Swiss eyelet makes the inner ruffle a Victorian delight. The pillow would also be pretty made with a pink ruffle as shown in the color drawing. *(continued)*

(continued)

Cutting Guide for One Block
Pieced block is 3½ x 3½"

☐ **Work with 6 cotton prints:**
  1 white-on-white floral print
  1 medium pink check or plaid
  4 pale floral calicos
  (Patterns for templates for the basic pieces are included, but these can easily be cut with a rotary cutter, if desired.)
☐ **From the white print cut:**
  1 strip 1 x 30"

4 pieces 1 x 2" (Pattern 3, page 52)
4 pieces 1 x 1" (Pattern 1, page 52)
☐ **From the medium print cut:**
  4 squares 1½ x 1½" (Pattern 2, page 52)
☐ **From another print cut:**
  1 strip 1 x 30"
  1 square 1 x 1" (Pattern 1, page 52)

Note: You will be cutting 16 small squares (Pattern 1 turned on point) from the two 30" strips after they have been stitched together. Therefore those strips can be in several sections if you are working with remnants or fat quarters.

¼" seam allowances are included in all dimensions and templates.

(continued)

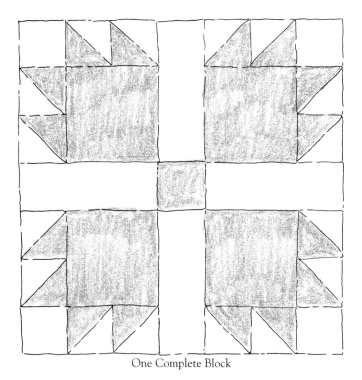

One Complete Block

Figure 1

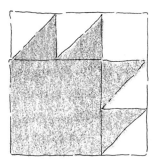

One Corner Unit

Figure 2

BLOCK CONSTRUCTION

The basic block consists of 4 corner units plus a center square and 4 rectangles as shown in **Figure 1**. A corner unit is shown in **Figure 2**.

To Make One Corner Unit

The pieces needed for one corner unit are shown in **Figure 3**. Drawn actual size, these pieces include the ¼" seam allowances and are laid in position for stitching.

Stitch the 1 x 30" medium pink plaid to the same size white print strip, right sides together, in a ¼" seam along the 30" length. Trim the seam allowance to ⅛" and press it toward the pink.

Trace **Pattern 1** onto plastic template material and carefully cut it out. Draw the corner-to-corner diagonal on the pattern.

Using **Figure 4** as a guide, place the template on the seamed pink and white strip with the diagonal line on the seam line. With a rotary cutter, cut out 16 pieces. (Spray a bit of adhesive on the back of the template to help hold it in place.)

Lay out the 6 pieces needed for a unit, placing them beside the machine in position as in **Figure 3.** Piece 3 is one of the 1-inch white squares cut from **Pattern 1.** Piece 6 is one of the 1½-inch squares cut from the medium print with **Pattern 2.** After each stitching step, press the seam and trim it to ⅛".

(continued)

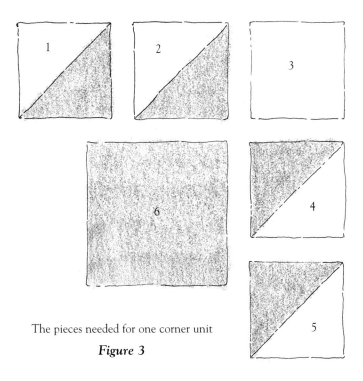

The pieces needed for one corner unit

Figure 3

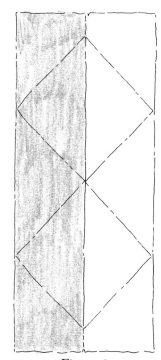

Figure 4

(continued)

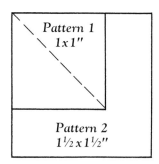

Pattern 1
1 x 1"

Pattern 2
1½ x 1½"

Pattern 3
1 x 2"

Seam pieces 1, 2, and 3 together. Seam pieces 4 and 5 together.

Stitch the joined 4 and 5 pieces to the side of 6.

Stitch the 1, 2, 3 piece to the top of the 4, 5, 6 piece. When pressed, the unit will look like **Figure 2.**

Make 3 more corner units.

To Complete the Block

Place the 4 corner units on a flat surface, placing them as in **Figure 1.** Position the center square **(Pattern 1)** and the 1 x 2" rectangles **(Pattern 3)** as shown. Stitch the pieces into 3 rows, then join the rows so the finished block looks like **Figure 1.**

CONSTRUCTING THE PILLOW TOP

Make 4 blocks. Press them well.

Following **Figure 5**, lay out the 4 blocks, the 4" lattice pieces, and the 1½" white square.

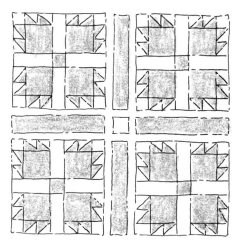

Layout for the Pillow Top
Figure 5

Join 2 blocks by stitching a 4x1½" lattice strip between them. Repeat with the other 2 blocks.

Stitch a 4x1½" lattice piece to the center 1½" white square, then join another lattice piece of the same size to the other side of the square.

Matching the seams carefully, stitch the lattice strip to a pair of blocks. Seam the other pair of blocks to the other side of the lattice strip.

After each step, trim the seam to ⅛" and press well.

Stitch one of the 2x8¾" lattice strips to each side of the piece. Trim the ends of the lattice pieces even with the piece if necessary.

Stitch a white corner block to one end of each of the other lattice pieces. Trim and press the seams.

Carefully measure the length of the lattice strip and stitch another white block at the other end so the seams will match the side lattice piece. Repeat for the other piece.

(continued)

Materials for Pillow

☐ **Cotton fabric in colors listed on page 48 for 4 blocks**
☐ **Pink cotton plaid: ½ yard**
☐ **White-on-white cotton print: ½ yard**
☐ **White eyelet edging, 3" wide: 2¾ yards**
☐ **Heirloom-weight batting 13x13"**
☐ **White cotton muslin for lining ¾ yard**
☐ **Polyester fiberfill to stuff pillow**
☐ **60-weight cotton mercerized sewing thread: white**
☐ **Transparent nylon thread for quilting**
☐ **Fine white cotton cord for piping 45"**

Cutting Guide For Pillow

Using the **Cutting Guide For One Block**, *cut the pieces specified to make 4 blocks. In addition, cut the following to complete the pillow:*

☐ **From the pink plaid:**
   the pillow back 13x13"
   4 lattice strips 2x8¾"
   4 lattice strips 4x1½"
☐ **From the white:**
   enough 8"-wide strips
   across the full width of
   the fabric to total 100"
   for ruffles (about 2½
   widths)
   1 square 1½ x1½"
   4 squares 2x2"
   enough 1"-wide bias
   strips to total 45"

(continued)

Stitch one strip to the top of the piece, the other to the bottom. Trim the seams and press. The piece will look like the color drawing of the pillow top without the ruffle.

QUILTING

Layer the quilt top, the batting, and one of the white muslin lining pieces. If the batting and lining are a bit larger than the top, leave the extra there until after quilting.

With transparent nylon thread on top and the white cotton in the bobbin, quilt "in the ditch" on all seam lines. Use a 2.5-mm length stitch.

In addition, quilt ¼" from the seam lines in the 4 white corner blocks and the 4 pink outside border pieces.

Trim the layers even, leaving a ¼" seam allowance.

MAKING THE PILLOW

Following the instructions on page 153, make 45" of corded piping.

Clipping the cording at the corners and matching the raw edges, stitch the piping to the outside of the pillow top.

Seam the three white ruffle strips together to make one long piece. Fold the piece in half to make a 4" wide piece.

Place the eyelet edging on top of the ruffle piece. Pin the raw edges together. Placing the rows ¼" apart, stitch 2 rows of gathering threads through the layered ruffle.

Taking care not to catch the thread ends, seam the ends of the piece, again making a tiny French seam.

Pull up the gathering threads to make the ruffle fit the pillow top. Pin it in place over the piping. Stitch.

Pin the remaining white muslin square to the wrong side of the pillow back as a lining.

With right sides together, seam the pillow back to the top, leaving one side partially open for turning.

Trim the seam. Turn right side out.

Fill with loose fiberfill. Stitch the opening closed with invisible stitches.

Victoria

◇

Beautiful, jewel-colored silks and metallic gold patches combine with a potpourri of embroidery to make a stocking Santa couldn't miss. Large enough to hold a generous array of trinkets, the stocking is made of typical Victorian crazy patches reduced in size so they measure just 2⅜" square. That makes some of the satiny pieces tiny—just big enough for a little silk rose.

An 8" square of each fabric is sufficient for each color. Check your remnant shelf for pretty, silky treasures. This stocking contains twelve fancy fabrics distributed among the twenty-one blocks needed to cut the stocking. The gold appears in every block and the black satin found its way into most, but otherwise the coloring is truly random. A luxurious black satin backing and the glorious ribbons on the cuff add their bit of Victorian finery to this whimsical creation.

Many crazy quilts were pieced from collected odds and ends, the squares sewn together without a pattern to take advantage of the fabrics, giving much variation to the blocks in the coverlet. A foundation pattern was used for the blocks in this stocking to make the stitching easy. Slight variations in the way the lines of the pattern are drawn and many variations in the way the fabrics are placed make for interesting architecture.

(continued)

Cutting Guide

☐ From the black satin cut:
  3 stockings
  1 rectangle 2½ x 8"
  2 pieces 1 x 8"
  Enough 1"-wide bias strips to total 2 yards
  Cut the small patches to fit as you stitch.

Materials

☐ **Black satin, 42" wide:** ½ yard
☐ **A collection of 10 to 12 silky fabrics:** gold lamé, red, green, teal, pink, rose, purple, medium blue, dark teal, dark green foulard print—8 x 8" of each
☐ **Some of the black satin**
☐ **Sheer muslin, 42" wide:** ¼ yard
☐ **Quilting fleece:**
  2 pieces 11 x 15"
  1 piece 2½ x 8½"
☐ **60-weight cotton mercerized thread:** black
☐ **A fancy gold and black hair bow or a collection of gold and black ribbons:** ½ yard pieces
☐ **Rayon embroidery thread:** 1 skein gold
☐ **Tiny ribbon rosebuds:** 7
☐ **Silk embroidery ribbon, 1-mm wide:** green, pink, blue, yellow, and red— several yards each
☐ **Six-strand embroidery floss:** small amounts in accent colors

(continued)

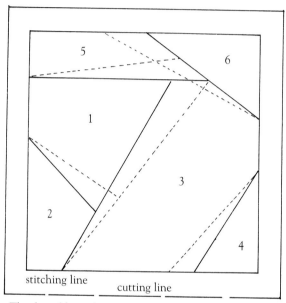

stitching line

cutting line

The dotted lines show minor variations for another block

Foundation Pattern for Crazy Quilt Block

MAKING A BLOCK

Muslin is better than paper for crazy patchwork since most of the fabrics are fragile and harder to handle than cotton. It also helps keep the piece intact during the embroidery. Choose a muslin that is fairly sheer so your pen marks will bleed through and be visible on both sides just in case you need help seeing the lines.

Trace the **Foundation Pattern for Crazy Quilt Block** onto the muslin to make 21 squares. Notice that on the pattern there are both solid stitching lines and a set of dotted lines. This second set of lines shows you how to move the ruler just slightly as you trace your patterns to create small variations in the blocks without redesigning or changing the stitching order. Trace one block using just the solid lines, then another using the dotted lines. After you have stitched two or three blocks, you may decide you want to make even bigger changes, as this can become really fun.

(continued)

(continued)

Cut the pieces of fabric as you need them.

Following the numbering sequence, make 21 blocks, stitching from either the right or wrong side of the pattern or use a combination of both. Place the colors randomly and avoid making two exactly alike. For continuity, use a bit of the gold and some of the black in each block. If the silky fabrics seem to be fraying too much, make the seam allowances a bit wider than the customary ⅛".

This is one time it is essential to add a final row of machine stitching just inside the cutting line to hold all those slippery pieces in place while you trim the edges and join them.

CONSTRUCTION OF THE STOCKING

Press the trimmed blocks lightly, working only on the wrong side.

Spread them out in 5 rows—3 rows of 4 blocks each and 2 rows of 3 blocks each as shown in **Figure 1**.

Stitch the black rectangle to this edge

Arrange the blocks into five rows placing them as shown

Figure 1

Arrange them in a pretty pattern. (The 3 extra blocks are for the stocking cuff.)

Making ¼" seams, stitch the blocks together. Do not trim the seams. Press open, again ironing only on the wrong side.

With right sides together, stitch the black satin rectangle to the top row of 3 blocks as noted in Figure 1. Press the seam toward the black.

Trace the **Stocking Pattern**, joining the pieces at the slashed line as directed. Cut the pattern out.

Place the pattern on the piece so the line joining the black satin to the patchwork matches the top of the pattern piece.

Remembering that no seam allowance is included on the pattern piece, pin the pattern to the blocks. (Note that there is a bit of extra length which can be used to make the stocking longer if you wish.)

Adding ¼" seam allowances all around, cut out the stocking. At the top, extend the cutting lines to the top of the black satin piece.

Using a zigzag stitch 4-mm wide with a 1-mm length, stitch around the stocking, placing the stitching right at the cut edge. This reinforcement protects the edges of the delicate fabrics while you embroider.

Place the cutout stocking on one of the 11x15" rectangles of fleece. Pin the two together. Using black thread, tie the two together at the points at which the squares join. Leave the rectangle of fleece untrimmed to protect the edges of the blocks while you embroider.

(continued)

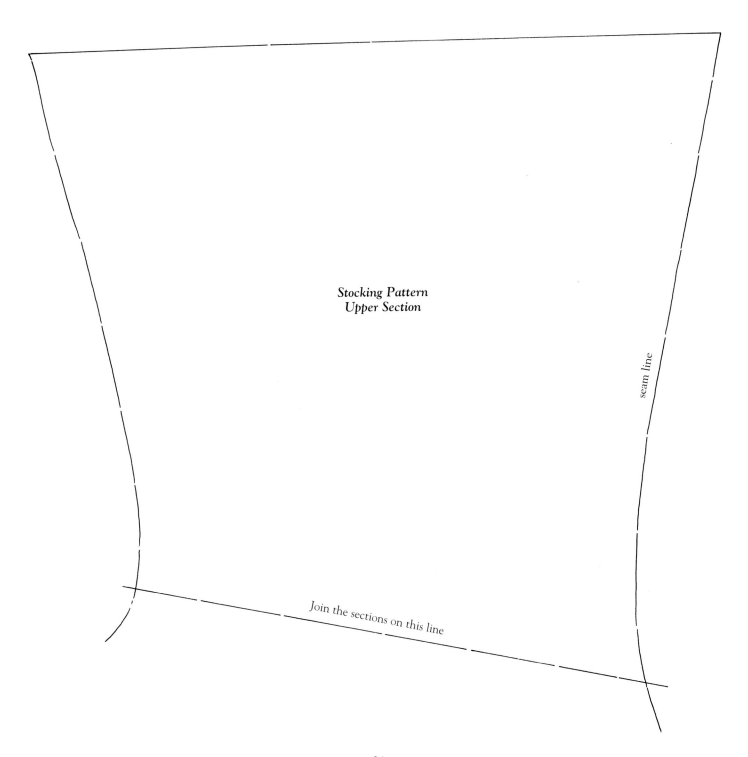

Stocking Pattern
Upper Section

seam line

Join the sections on this line

Join the sections on this line

Stocking Pattern
Lower Section

seam line

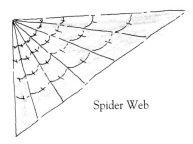

Spider Web

EMBROIDERY

Use the gold rayon thread to work a feather stitch outline around each block and every piece in the blocks. Let the stitching extend almost to the cut edges of the stocking piece to make sure the ends will be enclosed in the seam later.

The rest of the embroidery is rather random, depending usually on the maker's whim. In several of the triangular sections work a spiderweb in the gold thread. First place long threads radiating out from the point to the seam line. Cross these with 4 rows of fly stitches to hold the long threads in place so the finished web looks like the drawing in *Figure 2*.

Several blocks have little rosebuds made from silk ribbon and embroidery thread. To form them, make a flat stitch about ¼" long with the ribbon, placing it as shown in *Figure 2*. Then make a short straight stitch up from the base with green embroidery floss. Finish the

(continued)

Four-Petal Ribbon Flower

Ribbon
Rosebud

French Knot Flower

Bullion Knot
Rose

Ribbon Butterfly

Five-Petal
Ribbon Flower

Embroidery Ideas

Figure 2

bud with a green fly stitch at the bottom. Add the stem and lazy daisy leaves. Make some with two buds and some with three buds.

Attach purchased silk ribbon roses, scattering them evenly over the stocking. In several places, make a tiny ribbon bow. Attach bows to the fabric with sewing thread, then put silk roses on top.

Make another little rose with bullion knots. Place 1 knot wrapped about 7 times in the center, then make 2 knots wrapped about 10 times on each side of the center knot so they curve around it. Add two or three lazy daisy stitch leaves.

Four petals made with straight stitches of ribbon, centered with a French knot and 4 long straight stitches worked in embroidery floss make an easy flower.

Five ribbon petals made with a straight stitch and centered with a French knot form a slightly different flower.

A single yellow French knot made with embroidery floss and surrounded by a cluster of blue or pink French knots placed close together makes another sweet flower.

Make a little butterfly with flat ribbon stitches placed as shown in *Figure 2.* Use embroidery floss to make a bullion knot for a body and straight stitches for antennae.

Use your imagination for other trimmings. Victorians added all kinds of embellishments that you might already have—fancy buttons, gold or silver charms, beads, pearls, lace, and lace motifs to name just a few.

After you have completed the embroidery, trim the extra fleece around the stocking shape.

CUFF

Stitch the 3 blocks reserved for the cuff together in ¼" seams to make a long piece. Press the seams open.

Only a 1¾"-wide section of this piece will be used. Draw a line to

mark off that width and cut the piece.

Making a ¼" seam, stitch the two 1" black satin borders to the piece, one on each side. Press the seams toward the black. Back the cuff piece with the 2½x8" piece of fleece.

Embroider the patched portions of the cuff to match the rest of the stocking. A row of feather stitches along the black seams is a pretty finishing touch.

Following the instructions on page 153, make the 2 yards of corded piping.

Making ¼" seams, stitch cording to both black edges of the cuff.

With right sides together, stitch the cuff facing to one edge of the cuff. Turn the facing back and press.

Pin the faced cuff to the top of the patched stocking with the tops matching and the finished edge at the bottom.

Making a ¼" seam, stitch piping to the stocking shape, beginning at the top edge of the cuff and ending at the top edge on the other side.

BACKING

Pin an 11 x 15" rectangle of fleece to the wrong side of one of the three satin stockings. Using the black thread and a straight stitch 4-mm long, machine-quilt the piece in an overall diagonal pattern, placing the rows of stitching ½" apart.

Trim the fleece to the stocking shape.

With right sides together and making a ¼" seam, stitch the patched front to the quilted backing. Clip the seam allowance at the curves. Turn right side out.

For a hanging loop, make a 3"-long twisted cord of black embroidery floss and attach the ends to the top of the stocking on the heel side.

LINING

With right sides together, stitch the two remaining satin stocking shapes with a ¼" seam beginning and ending at the top edge.

Slip the lining into the stocking. Allowing the hanging loop to extend upward, turn the raw edges to the inside and stitch together with small invisible stitches.

BOW

The most interesting part of the bow shown on the stocking is a fancy gold and black holiday hair ornament. It consists of a black silk flower with gold beads, gold mesh ribbon, twisted black satin cord, black satin tubing, and three varieties of gold metallic cord. These are everywhere at Christmas time, but you can assemble something similar if you prefer.

The purchased bow was attached to a larger bow made of gold and black striped wire-edged ribbon to make an extravagant trim for the stocking in true Victorian tradition.

Tiny Trees

The very size of the miniature quilt makes it perfect for holiday decorating. It can be designed in colors to coordinate with the rest of your trimmings, stitched quickly, and combined with a collection of old favorites to make all seem new and fresh.

Fabric designers in the last few years have been creating vibrant Christmas prints with jewel-like colors and beautiful motifs that have their roots in tradition, yet are thoroughly new. Some prints have parts of the design highlighted with a gold wash to add sparkle and a festive mood. Angels, bells, bows, endearing animals, antique toys, and vintage Santas adorn many of the prints.

One of the new prints used as the basis for the trees and one of the borders in this quilt is a patchwork of little squares and rectangles printed in a mélange of coordinating designs. Since miniatures take such little pieces of fabric for patches, cutting the trees from the various prints in the patchwork made it possible to have scores of different but compatible prints without buying more than the one piece of fabric. Miniature makers develop an eye for that kind of treasure!

This quilt is finished with a combination of hand and machine quilting. Transparent thread used for machine stitching "in the ditch" is almost invisible while delicate hand stitching inside the blocks creates the illusion of a piece quilted entirely by hand. *(continued)*

Materials

- ☐ **Christmas patchwork cotton print, 42" wide: ⅜ yard**
- ☐ **A red-background Christmas cotton print that coordinates with the patchwork: ¼ yard**
- ☐ **Cream tone-on-tone cotton print, 42" wide: ½ yard**
- ☐ **Gray tone-on-tone cotton print: 6x6"**
- ☐ **Gold cotton print: 6x6"**
- ☐ **Small cotton cord: 66"**
- ☐ **Traditional quilt batting: 16x18"**
- ☐ **60-weight cotton mercerized thread: off-white**
- ☐ **60-weight cotton mercerized thread: to match the print fabrics**
- ☐ **Transparent nylon quilting thread**

Cutting Guide

Most pieces can be cut as you go, but to ensure that there is fabric for the large pieces, cut first:

- ☐ **From the cream tone-on-tone fabric:**
  the quilt back 15x17"
  1 strip 2½x25"
  2 strips 1½x10½"
  2 strips 1½x8½"
- ☐ **From each of the 2 Christmas prints:**
  2 strips 1½x10½"
  2 strips 1½x8½"

From one of the prints, cut: enough 1"-wide bias strips to total 66"

◇

(continued)

THE LITTLE TREE BLOCKS

BLOCK IS 2 X 2"

Copy the **Foundation Pattern for Trees** 10 times.

Cut the pieces for the trees from

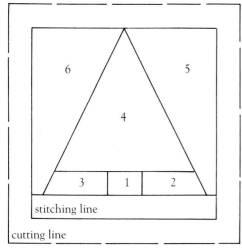

Foundation Pattern for Trees

the little Christmas prints in the patchwork design. The trees can all be cut from the same print, or they can be a mixture of prints as in the pictured quilt. Use the gray print fabric for the tree trunks; the cream tone-on-tone print is used for the background (the pieces marked 2, 3,

5, and 6 on the tree foundation pattern).

Stitch the fabrics together on the paper in the numbered order. Make 10 tree blocks. Press. Leave the paper in the blocks.

THE TREE TRUNK BLOCKS

BLOCK IS 2 X 2"

Make two 4–patch blocks like the ones shown at the base of the tree in **Figure 1**. Cut a strip of the gray tone-on-tone fabric 1½ x 4". Cut the

The Tree Panel

Figure 1

tone-on-tone cream colored fabric the same size. Stitch the two together along the 6" length, making a ¼" seam.

Cut 2 strips of print fabrics 1½ x 4". Stitch these together in a ¼" seam as for the gray and cream strip.

Press both strips and trim the seam allowances to ⅛". Press the seam allowance toward the gray fabric on the gray and cream strip.

From each strip cut 2 pieces 1½" wide, cutting vertically across the seam line. (You'll have a bit extra in case the ends aren't as perfect as you would wish.)

Place the pieces as shown in **Figure 2**. Stitch the horizontal seams to make two 4-patch blocks. Trim the seams to ⅛" and press.

(continued)

The Four Patch Tree Trunk Blocks

Figure 2

(continued)

Still holding the sections as in **Figure 2,** stitch the two 4-patch blocks together in a ¼" seam. Trim the seam and press.

ASSEMBLING THE TREE PANEL

Lay out the 10 trees in 4 rows, as shown on **Figure 1.**

Place the joined tree trunk blocks under the trees as indicated in **Figure 1.**

Cut the 2½ x 25" strip of cream fabric into 16 pieces 2½ x 1½". These are the background pieces for the edges of the tree panel.

Following **Figure 1,** stitch together the horizontal rows of trees and background pieces. The top row consists of 3 background rectangles, 1 tree, and 3 more background pieces. The others follow in sequence as on the drawing. As each row is stitched, press the seams and trim to ⅛". Leave the paper behind the tree pieces until you are instructed to remove it.

Matching the seams carefully, stitch the 5 horizontal rows together into one panel.

THE NINE-PATCH BORDER BLOCKS
BLOCK IS 3 X 3"

Cut 10 print squares 1½ x 1½" and cut 8 cream-colored squares the same size. Lay them out as in **Figure 3**, arranging the prints in a pattern that pleases you.

The Nine-Patch Border Block
Figure 3

Join the squares to make 3 strips. Trim the seams and press.

Join the horizontal rows to make a 9-patch block. Make a second block. Trim the seams and press.

THE STAR BORDER BLOCKS
BLOCK IS 3 X 3"

Figure 4 shows an entire star block. The foundation pattern is for one-eighth of the block—the portion of Figure 4 shown in color. To complete one block, make 8 sections. These little three-piece sections are quick and easy.

To begin, copy the **Foundation Pattern for Star** 16 times.

If you are using the suggested colors, use the cream-colored background fabric for piece 1, a gold print for piece 2, and the red print for piece 3. Stitch them together on the paper in numerical order. Make certain the pieces are cut large enough to extend to the cutting line.

Make 8 sections placing the fabric on the wrong side of the foundation drawings. Then turn the papers over and work on the right side of the remaining 8 foundation patterns to make 8 sections that are mirror images of the first.

Join 8 sections to make the star design as shown in Figure 4. Press. Make the second, mirror-image star. Leave the paper in the blocks.

The Border

Join 1 cream-colored and 2 print 10½" border pieces along their long edges to make a strip, placing the cream on one side and the two prints next to each other. (See the color drawing of the quilt on page 69.) Trim the seams and press. Repeat for the other 10½" pieces and the 1½ x 8½" pieces to make three more borders.

Stitch the longer border pieces to the sides of the quilt panel with the cream sides joining the panel. Trim the seams and press.

Stitch the star blocks to the ends of one 8½" border. Trim the seams

(continued)

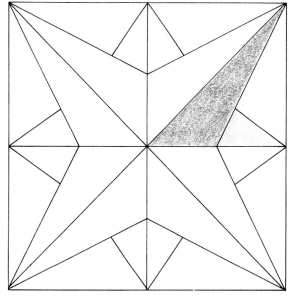

The Star Border Block

Figure 4

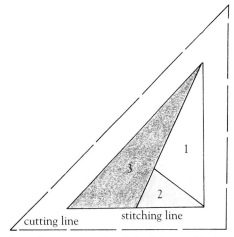

cutting line   stitching line

This foundation makes ⅛th of the star block

Foundation Pattern for Star

(continued)

and press. Stitch this border to the top of the quilt. Trim and press the seam.

Stitch the 9-patch blocks to the ends of the remaining border piece. Trim the seams and press. Stitch this border to the bottom edge of the quilt. Again trim the seam and press. The unhemmed piece measures 15 x 17".

FINISHING

Following the instructions on page 153, make 66" of corded piping from one of the prints. Trim the seam allowance of the piping to ¼".

With raw edges matching, stitch the piping to the outside of the quilt top.

Remove the paper from the backs of the blocks.

Press the top well. Layer the quilt back, the batting, and the top, smoothing out any wrinkles. Pin them together.

Using transparent nylon thread on top and off-white 60-weight cotton

in the bobbin, quilt "in the ditch" around every piece of patchwork. Begin and end the stitching ⅝" from the edges so you will be able to turn the raw edges to the inside to finish the quilt.

Since the actual stitches of the machine quilting are almost invisible, the addition of hand quilting in the places where it is most apparent gives the illusion of an all-hand-quilted piece with much less time required.

Use the off-white cotton thread in the cream areas and dark matching thread in the print portions of the design to hand-quilt a scant ¼" inside each patch. Follow the quilting lines—the very light lines—on the color drawing of the quilt for placement of these hand stitches.

After all quilting is complete, trim the outside edges even. Cut away an additional ¼" of the batting and turn the seam allowance to the inside and fasten it with small invisible stitches.

Finish quilting at the edges.

A Winter's Night

FALLING SNOW BRINGS THOUGHTS OF HOME

FINISHED SIZE: 16¾ x 21¼"

(continued)

*F*abrics are the story behind this cozy little quilt, which would be pretty as a wall hanging or on a doll bed. When cut into small pieces, a blue batik-like print becomes sky filled with snowflakes or stars. Reproduction red calico adds a textured look to little houses while six different cream-colored prints stitched into log cabin blocks form borders that are puffy and delicately shaded. The gray roofs are cut from a large feather-patterned print. The green-on-green floral print makes wonderful trees and grass.

The tone-on-tone prints come in a wide array of floral, geometric, and abstract patterns. Choose three that all have a muslin background, but different amounts of white added for the pattern. Find another group of three prints with the same muslin background with cream or beige patterns printed on them. Little contrast is needed to create the lightly shaded borders.

Materials

- ☐ **Red cotton print: ⅜ yard**
- ☐ **Green cotton print: ½ yard**
- ☐ **Blue batik-like cotton print: ¼ yard**
- ☐ **Gray cotton print: 8 x 8"**
- ☐ **3 different light cream tone-on-tone cotton prints: ⅛ yard each**
- ☐ **3 different darker cream tone-on-tone cotton prints: ⅛ yard each**
- ☐ **Light gray cotton print: 3 x 3"**
- ☐ **Cotton muslin backing: 17 x 22"**
- ☐ **Cotton cording: 2¼ yards**
- ☐ **Transparent nylon quilting thread**
- ☐ **50-weight cotton mercerized thread: ecru for construction and quilting**
- ☐ **Fine point, nonbleeding, permanent black fabric marker or pen**

Cutting Guide

- ☐ **From the red print cut:**
  2 pieces 2¼ x 13¼"
  2 pieces 2¼ x 20½"
- ☐ **From the green print cut:**
  2 strips 1 x 12¼"
  2 strips 1 x 19"
  Enough 1"-wide bias strips to total 82"
- ☐ **From the blue batik-like print cut:**
  2 strips ¾ x 11½"
  2 strips ¾ x 8¼"

Cut the other pieces as you stitch. Note: Seam allowances throughout are ¼".

THE LITTLE HOUSE BLOCKS

BLOCK IS 2¾ X 2¾"

Each house block is constructed by stitching together the 5 **Foundation Patterns for House**. Copy them 7 times and make 7 house blocks following the instructions below. For the time being, ignore the details shown on the door and window pieces.

Cut the little pieces as you stitch. Place each color as noted on the foundation patterns and stitch in the numbered order.

Beginning with the chimney piece and using the pieces in the order that the foundation patterns have been placed on the page, stitch the five pieces together to make the house. Press the seams open. Leave the paper in the blocks.

With the fabric marker, draw in the window and the door details as shown on the foundation patterns. Do this freehand and don't try for absolute accuracy. Slight variations add to the charm of the piece.

(continued)

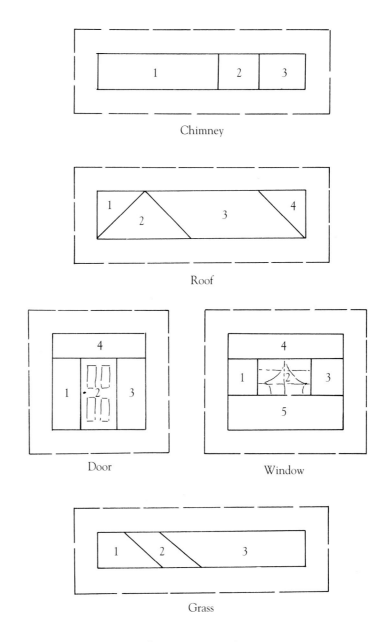

Chimney

Roof

Door

Window

Grass

Foundation Patterns for House

(continued)

THE TREE BLOCKS

BLOCK IS 1⅝ X 1⅝"

Copy the **Foundation Pattern for Tree** 6 times.

Use the colors as noted on the pattern and stitch in the numbered order. Make 6 tree blocks.

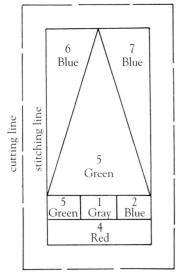

Foundation Pattern for Tree

THE SMALL LOG CABIN BLOCKS

BLOCK IS 1⅝ X 1⅝"

Although these blocks are essentially one color, the assortment of prints reflects light differently to create a texture that gives the blocks depth. Decide the placement of the prints and make all the blocks alike following the light and dark notations on the pattern. Use only 5 of the prints in these blocks.

Copy the **Foundation Pattern for Small Log Cabin Block** 36 times (28 blocks for the border, 8 for the center panel).

Stitch in the numbered order using the light- and dark-toned prints as noted on the foundation pattern.

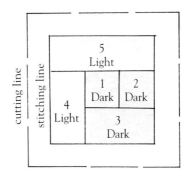

Foundation Pattern for Small Log Cabin Block

LARGE LOG CABIN BLOCKS

BLOCK IS 2¾ X 2¾"

Trace the **Foundation Pattern for Large Log Cabin Block** and make 16 copies.

Sort the cream tone-on-tone prints into light and dark.

Use the light and dark notations on the pattern to guide placement. Use the lightest of the darks for pieces 2, 4, and 5. Then move outward following the numbered sequence. The block will be shaded like the foundation pattern. Make 16 blocks. *(continued)*

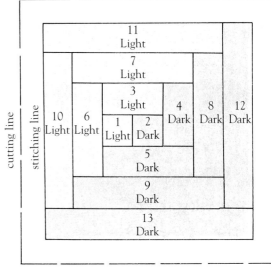

Foundation Pattern for Large Log Cabin Block

◇

(continued)

ASSEMBLING THE CENTER PANEL

Using *Figure 1* as a guide, stitch together a house and 2 tree blocks with the house block in the middle. Make 3 strips like this.

The Center Panel

Figure 1

Stitch together 4 of the small Log Cabin blocks. Make 2 of these strips.

Beginning with a house strip, stitch together the Log Cabin and house strips to make a center panel like *Figure 1.* Press the seams open.

THE INNER LOG CABIN BORDER

Make 2 strips of 8 small Log Cabin blocks. Press the seams open and stitch them to the sides of the center panel.

Stitch together blocks to make 2 strips of 6 blocks each.

Stitch the strips to the top and bottom of the panel. Press all seams open. The panel measures 7¼ x 11½". Leave the paper in the piece.

BLUE BORDER

Stitch the two ¾ x 11½" blue batik-like print strips to the side edges of the panel, making ¼" seams.

Stitch the two ¾ x 8¼" blue batik-like print strips to the top and bottom of the panel in ¼" seams. Press the seams toward the blue.

LOG CABIN BORDER

Placing all the blocks with their dark sides to the top and outside edges, stitch 5 large Log Cabin blocks together to make a vertical strip like the one in *Figure 2*. Make 2.

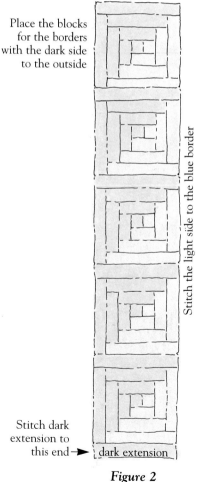

Place the blocks for the borders with the dark side to the outside

Stitch the light side to the blue border

Stitch dark extension to this end → dark extension

Figure 2

Cut 4 pieces of the darkest print 1 x 2¼".

Stitch 1 of these pieces to the short light end of each strip as noted on Figure 2.

Stitch the long light edge of the strip to the blue batik-like border.

Stitch 3 large Log Cabin blocks together, again placing them so the dark edges are to the outside. Stitch 1 of the dark print pieces to the light end as for the side border pieces. Make 2.

Stitch a house block to each end of the strips.

Stitch these to the top and bottom edges of the piece. The panel measures 12¼ x 16½".

OUTER BORDER

Stitch the two 1 x 12¼" strips of green to the top and bottom of the panel, making ¼" seams. Press the seams toward the green.

Stitch the 2 dark green 1 x 19" strips to the sides of the piece in ¼" seams and press the seams toward the green.

Making ¼" seams as before, stitch the two 2¼ x 13¼" red print strips to the top and bottom of the piece. Press the seams toward the red.

Stitch the 2 red 2¼ x 20½" strips to the sides of the panel with ¼" seams and press the seams toward the red.

FINISHING

Following the instructions on page 153, make 82" of piping using the green 1" bias strips. Trim the seam allowance on the piping to ¼".

Matching the raw edges, stitch the piping to the outside edges of the red border.

Layer the muslin quilt backing, the batting, and the quilt top. Smooth out any wrinkles. Pin together.

With transparent nylon thread on top, 50-weight off-white cotton thread in the bobbin, and a 2.5-mm stitch length, machine-quilt "in the ditch" as follows: around each house and tree block, both sides of the blue and red borders, and between the large Log Cabin blocks in the border.

Trim the batting and backing even with the edges of the top. Take an extra ¼" off the batting.

Turn the raw edges to the inside and fasten with invisible stitches.

Barrie's Vest

Little girls love to dress up, and a quilted vest made to match a pretty dress becomes a favorite accessory, fun to wear with a dress but also great with a shirt and jeans. The use of a lightweight traditional quilt batting and machine quilting control the bulk usually found in quilted clothing, making this a wonderful, wearable gift.

The picture block used for the vest front makes it possible to take small motifs from large designs and use them in a unique way. For the vest, a cute Victorian teddy bear print on a black background was cut to use as the center picture, then surrounded with other more sophisticated prints and the check from the dress to create a new fabric with a personality all its own.

The vest shown is a size four. The materials listed should be sufficient for a classic fitted vest up to a size six, but keeping in mind that patterns vary, use the materials list as a guide only. Depending on the cut of your pattern and the size being made, you may have to add a row of blocks to the pieces you make.

The dress photographed with the vest has a traditional fitted bodice with a natural waistline, gathered skirt, and puffed sleeves. The bodice, sleeves, and collar were made from a tucked white batiste fabric. The skirt is a cotton quilter's fabric. Using the same fabric for the vest lining, the blocks, the skirt, and the trim on the collar and sleeves ties the pieces together as an outfit.

(continued)

Materials

- ☐ **Dark cotton print for sashing, block corners, and vest back, 44" wide:** ½ yard
- ☐ **Checked cotton fabric for vest lining and use in blocks, 44" wide:** ½ yard
- ☐ **Bright blue cotton print:** 12x12"
- ☐ **Picture cotton fabric:** ¼ yard
- ☐ **Traditional quilt batting:** 20x26"
- ☐ **Pattern for classic tailored vest**
- ☐ **50-weight cotton mercerized thread for construction:** black
- ☐ **Transparent nylon thread for machine quilting**

Cutting Guide

- ☐ **From the dark print, cut:**
  the vest back
  24 strips 1¼ x 3½"
  8 strips 1¼ x 13"
  Enough 1"-wide bias strips to total 2½ yards
- ☐ **From the checked fabric, cut** the lining front and back
- ☐ **Cut the small strips for the blocks as you sew**

(continued)

THE PICTURE BLOCK

Copy the **Foundation Pattern for the Picture Block** 18 times and make 18 blocks following the numbered stitching order. Note that the blocks have been set on point for the vest front and orient the chosen picture with that in mind.

The teddy bear print contained other Victorian toy illustrations. Some were placed so close to the bears that is was not possible to cut a bear without a bit of color from another toy as part of the background. This is usually not a problem since only a part of the other toy is contained in the cutout. These little bits just become interesting variations of color in the background.

THE VEST FRONT

Lay 9 of the blocks in a diamond shape as shown in **Figure 1**. Join the diagonal rows by inserting the 3½" strips of the dark print as shown by the light blue pieces on Figure 1.

Using the 13" strips—shown as dark blue in **Figure 1**—join the rows and finish the outside edges of the square with the dark print.

Repeat to make another piece.

Remove the paper from the backs of the blocks. Press.

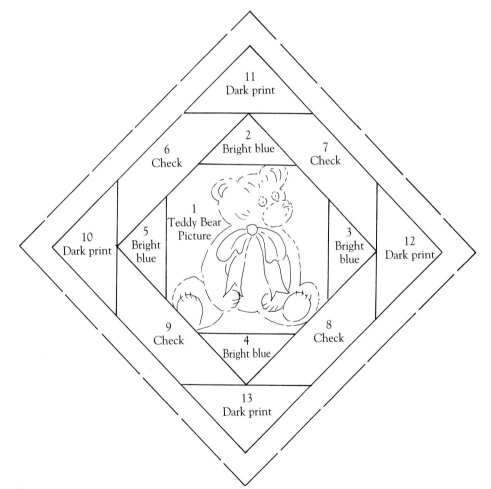

Foundation Pattern for the Picture Block

Assembling the Vest

Place the pattern for the vest front on the piece as shown in **Figure 2**. As noted on page 80, your pattern may vary enough that it is necessary to add a row of blocks to cut your vest.

Cut out the vest fronts, remembering to reverse the pattern to make a right and a left front.

Disregarding the pattern construction directions, stitch the vest fronts to the back at the shoulders. Repeat for the lining. Press the seams open.

Using the lining as a pattern, cut the batting.

Layer the lining, the batting and the pieced vest. Pin together carefully.

(continued)

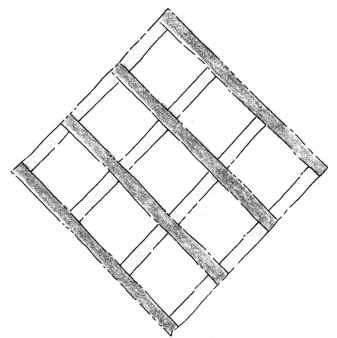

The 3½" sashing strips are shown as light blue

Figure 1

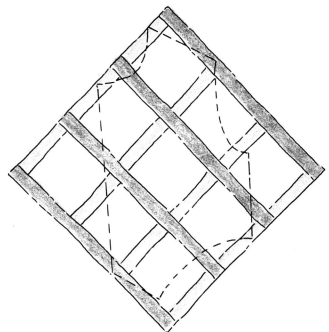

Place the pattern on the pieced diamond

Figure 2

(continued)

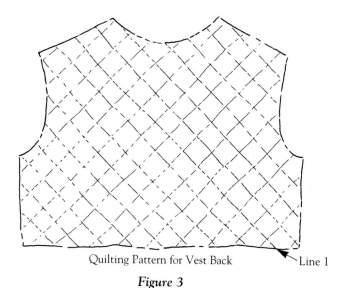

Quilting Pattern for Vest Back

Figure 3

QUILTING

Using the transparent nylon thread on the top and the black cotton thread in the bobbin, machine-quilt the vest. Follow *Figure 3* for the easy diagonal design for the back. To start the diagonal pattern, place a piece of 1"-wide masking tape across the vest back from the shoulder seam to the lower edge as shown by Line 1 on the diagram. Stitch along both sides of the tape, then move the tape so one edge is against one of the rows of stitching.

Stitch the next line, then move the tape so the edge is against a row of stitching. Complete all stitching in one direction.

Repeat the process in the opposite direction.

Quilt the front "in the ditch" along the lines made by the sashing strips. Additionally, stitch around the picture of the bear. (Quilting was not done along all the piecing lines because the additional stitching would detract from the softly puffed feeling of the vest photographed.)

(continued)

(continued)

FINISHING

Stitch the front to the back at the underarms using the seam allowance suggested by the pattern. Trim the seam to ¼" and press open.

Cut a 1"-wide strip of lining fabric. Press under a scant ¼" of the raw edge on each side and whipstitch the strip over the seam to cover the raw edges.

Join the bias strips that were cut from the dark print fabric to make one continuous piece 2½ yards long.

Trim the seam allowance on the armholes and the outside edge of the vest so they are exactly ¼" wide.

With right sides together and matching the raw edges, stitch the binding to the edges in a ¼" seam.

Turn the bias to the wrong side, pulling it against the batting so there is a neat ¼" edge, and pin the bias in place on the wrong side. Turn the raw edge under and stitch it by hand to the lining with tiny invisible stitches.

Quilted Kitties

◆

(continued)

(continued)

The first little girl who saw this sweater loved the "kitty-cat necklace" appliquéd to the front and wanted to try it on immediately. Children love playful designs like this quick pieced and quilted miniature block and so adults fondly stitch them. After making one easy block, you'll see other uses for the design—a row of kittens across the brim of a warm winter cap, marching in a row across the top of a cuddly crib quilt and edging nursery curtains to match, on a pocket or overalls bib—anywhere that would make a little one smile.

The appliqué has been applied only to the front of the sweater, leaving the soft ease of sweater dressing in tact. This means that only five kitten blocks are needed, making this a speedy project for most quilters. The impish embroidered faces employ simple stitches and are a special touch that adds whimsical charm to the piece.

Materials
- [ ] **Light blue cotton fabric, 44" wide: ¼ yard**
- [ ] **White–on–white cotton print fabric: 12 x 12"**
- [ ] **Six-strand embroidery floss: several yards each of blue, pink, gray, and black**
- [ ] **Quilter's fleece: 13 x 10"**
- [ ] **60-weight cotton mercerized thread: white for construction**
- [ ] **Transparent nylon thread for quilting**
- [ ] **White cotton cording, very small: 1 yard**
- [ ] **White sweater**

Foundation Pattern for Kitten Face

Cutting Guide

☐ **From the blue fabric cut:**

first, a piece 9 x 13" for
the facing

Then 5 sashing strips:

1¼ x 2½"

1 strip 1¼ x 5¾"

1 strip 1¼ x 8¼"

2 strips 1¼ x 9"

Enough 1"-wide bias strips
to total 37"

Cut the small blue and white
patches for the blocks as you stitch.

THE KITTEN BLOCKS

Trace the **Foundation Pattern for Kitten Face**, including the facial features. Copy it so you have 5 foundations.

Following the numbered stitching order and using the colors as suggested, stitch 5 blocks.

Hold the block to a window or light box and trace the facial features through from the pattern.

Remove the paper from behind the large face section, leaving the balance in place. With a single strand of embroidery floss in a size 6 crewel needle, embroider the face. Use blue satin stitches for the eyes and pink satin stitches for the nose, placing the stitches horizontally for both. Gray outline stitches make the whisker and eyelashes and outline the eyes. A single long stitch made with 2 strands of black placed on top of the satin stitches makes cat-like pupils.

Embroider all 5 blocks.

(continued)

◇

(continued)

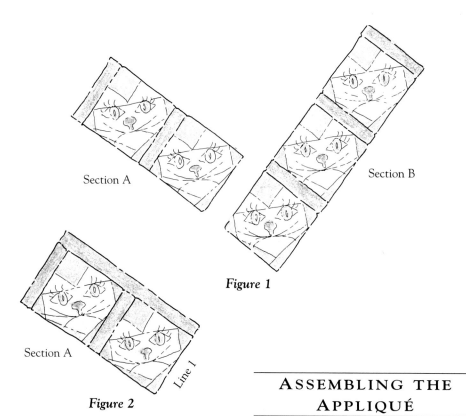

Section A

Section B

Figure 1

Section A

Line 1

Figure 2

Section B

Line 1

Figure 3

ASSEMBLING THE APPLIQUÉ

Using 2 of the 1¼ x 2½" blue sashing strips, stitch together 2 kitten blocks with a sashing strip between them and one at the top end to make Section A as shown in ***Figure 1***. Press the seams toward the sashing strips throughout the assembly. The blue sashing pieces are shown on the drawings as gray to help with construction.

Following the drawing for Section B and placing the sashing strips as shown, stitch together 3 kitten blocks and three 1¼ x 2½" sashing strips to construct Section B.

Stitch the 1¼ x 5¾" sashing strip to the top of Section A as shown in ***Figure 2***. Press.

Stitch the 1¼ x 8¼" strip to the top of section B as shown in ***Figure 3***. Press.

Stitch Section A to Section B along Line 1 to make the V-shaped piece. Press.

Allowing the extra length to extend at the point, stitch the 1¼ x 9" strips to the bottom edge of piece, ending the seams ¼" before the point. Press with extensions out flat.

Fold the top extension back so it makes a miter and press in the fold.

Using the fold line as a guide, stitch the two extensions into a seam. Trim the seam to ¼" and press. The piece now looks like the color drawing shown on the sweater neck.

Remove the paper from the blocks. Press.

FINISHING

Join the 1"-wide bias strips to make one continuous piece, and following the instruction on page 153, make 37" of corded piping. Trim the seam allowances to ¼".

Beginning and ending at a top corner, stitch the piping to the right side of the V-shaped piece, matching the raw edges and mitering the corners so it lays flat.

Use the assembled V-shaped piece as a pattern to cut a lining from the 9 x 13" blue fabric and a piece of quilt batting.

Lay the three pieces flat with the backing on the bottom, wrong side up. Follow with the batting, then the pieced V right side up. Pin the layers together.

Using the nylon quilting thread, stitch "in the ditch" along the sashing strips and to outline the kitten faces. Stop stitching ¼" before

the points where the stitching would intersect the piping to allow the raw edges to be turned to the inside later.

Trim away ¼" along the edges of the batting.

Carefully turn the raw edges to the inside and whipstitch them together to finish the piece.

Pin the appliqué to the sweater, placing it as shown on the color drawing. Using invisible stitches, stitch the piece to the sweater.

Memories

◇

Many quilters love scrap quilts best. Not only does our joy in creating "something from nothing" flourish with these wonderful and unique quilts, but using the tiny leftovers from favorite clothing brings back so many happy memories. It is a quiet pleasure to sort scraps remembering the little girl who wore the dress printed with red cherries, the dimpled boy in the yellow rompers, the tomboy hanging from the tree while the plaid shirt dangled to almost hide her laughing face, the legendary apple pies mother baked wearing the pink calico apron, and the shy little girl who went so bravely to the first day of kindergarten in a smocked dress of the pale blue muslin.

Many of the traditional quilt patterns adapt well to the scrap concept. The Bow Tie has always been one of these. Since it is also a good one for the miniature size, it is ideal for a doll quilt made from scraps of a little girl's favorite clothing. Choosing medium-to-light-hued fabrics and a Swiss eyelet ruffle, uniting them with an unbleached

muslin background, and lightly antiquing all with a coffee "dye" makes a doll quilt that becomes a cherished toy. Even all new fabrics could be used this way to make an "antique" to grace the doll cradle.

While the pieces of fabric needed to assemble the blocks for this quilt are small, they are easy to handle.

This one can be constructed without a foundation pattern. While patterns to make templates for cutting the squares of fabric are included on page 97, you may find it just as easy to cut the pieces with a rotary cutter.

(continued)

Materials

- ☐ 15 assorted cotton print pieces: each 5 x 2⅛"
- ☐ 1 cotton print for inside border: 2 x 42"
- ☐ Unbleached cotton muslin, 42" wide: ¾ yard
- ☐ Cotton eyelet edging, 3" wide: 4 yards ecru
- ☐ Low-loft heirloom batting: 18 x 20"
- ☐ 60-weight cotton mercerized thread: off-white for construction and quilting

Cutting Guide

- ☐ **From each 5 x 2⅛" print piece cut:** 4 squares 1¼ x 1¼" (Pattern 1) 4 squares ⅞ x ⅞" (Pattern 2)
- ☐ **From the border print cut:** 2 strips 1 x 10½" 2 strips 1 x 13½"
- ☐ **From the muslin cut:** the quilt backing 18 x 20" 60 squares 1¼ x 1¼" (Pattern 1) 20 lattice strips 1 x 2" 7 horizontal lattice strips 1 x 9½" 2 vertical frame pieces 1 x 12½" 2 border pieces 3 x 11½" 2 border pieces 3 x 19½"

◇

(continued)

ASSEMBLING ONE BOW TIE BLOCK

BLOCK IS 2 X 2"

One complete block as shown by the **Bow Tie** drawing is made from 2 unbleached muslin 1¼" squares, 2 print 1¼" squares, and 2 print ⅞" squares. The print squares should be cut from the same fabric.

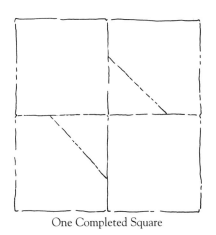

One Completed Square

Bow Tie

With right sides together, stitch a small print square to a muslin square, holding the pieces as shown in **Figure 1**. Match the raw edges as shown and stitch in a diagonal line from corner to corner on the small square.

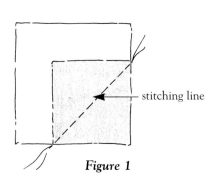

stitching line

Figure 1

Trim the seam to ⅛" and press. Make 2. The wrong side of these two squares looks like **Figure 2**.

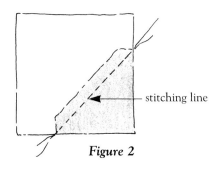

stitching line

Figure 2

Match the outside edges of one pieced square to the edges of a 1¼" print square as shown in **Figure 3**. (The print piece in the drawing is

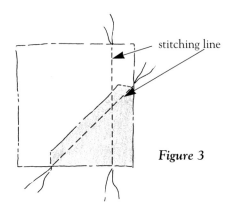

stitching line

Figure 3

underneath and not visible.) Stitch a ¼" seam as shown. Trim the seam allowance to ⅛". Press. Repeat to make 1 more section.

Place the 2 pieces as shown in **Figure 4**. With right sides together, stitch them along the line A-B. Trim the seam and press. The little finished block should measure 2 x 2" including the seam allowances on all sides. *(continued)*

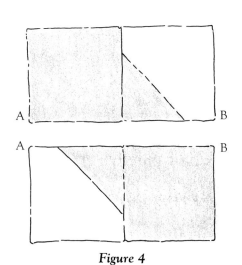

Figure 4

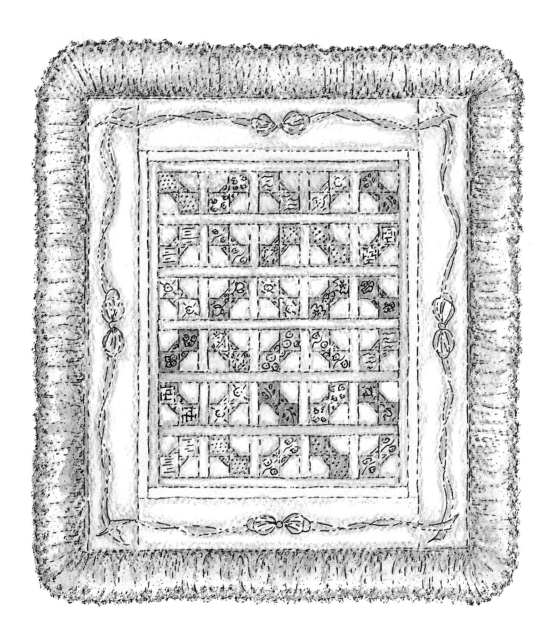

(continued)

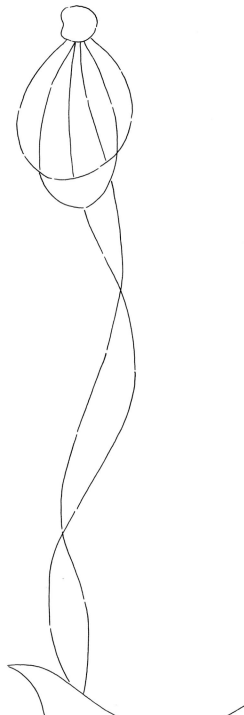

ASSEMBLING THE PIECED TOP

Following the procedure for assembling the blocks, make 30 blocks. Since there are 15 different prints, you will be making 2 using each print.

Lay the little squares on a flat surface and arrange them in 6 rows of 5 each, taking into consideration distribution of color and prints. Notice on the color drawing of this quilt that the blocks have been set so the bows are diagonal and that the slant alternates across the rows. Your bows could all slant in the same direction if you wish.

Beginning and ending with Bow Tie squares, join the blocks into 6 rows by stitching the 1 x 2" lattice strips to the sides of the squares. Trim all seams to ⅛" and press as each row is completed.

Join the 6 horizontal rows with five 1 x 9½" muslin lattice strips. Use the 2 remaining lattice strips at the top and bottom of the piece. Again trim all seams and press.

Stitch the 2 muslin 1 x 12½" vertical frame pieces to the sides. Trim the seams and press.

THE BORDERS

Stitch the 1 x 10½" print border pieces to the top and bottom of the piece. Trim the seams and press.

Stitch the two 1 x 13½" print border pieces to the sides of the piece. Trim the seams and press.

Add the muslin outer border, stitching the 3 x 11½" pieces to the top and bottom first and following with the 3 x 19½" side pieces. As before, trim the seams and press as the stitching is done. The finished quilt top should measure 17½ x 19".

Bow Quilting Design

FINISHING

Fold the quilt top and mark the center of each of the outer muslin borders.

Trace the **Bow Quilting Design** with a heavy line. Center the knot of the border bows at the marked center of the muslin borders and trace the quilting design.

Layer the muslin quilt backing, the batting, and the quilt top, smoothing out any wrinkles. Pin the layers together securely. Baste if you wish, but it is possible to machine-quilt this little piece without that step.

With the cotton thread, machine-quilt "in the ditch" on all seams. Tie off the thread ends and bury them in the batting.

Join the ends of the eyelet ruffle piece in a small French seam and gather it to fit the outside edge of the quilt. Add extra fullness at the corners so the ruffle will lie flat.

Holding the batting and lining out of the way, stitch the gathered eyelet to the quilt top. Trim the seam and turn the raw edges to the inside. Fasten with small invisible stitches.

Using the off-white cotton thread, quilt the bow design in the border by hand or machine. (Doing this by hand is a beautiful touch that makes the quilt look as if it has all been hand-quilted since the machine stitching has all disappeared "in the ditch.")

If you wish to antique the quilt with a coffee dye solution—see page 158 for directions—slightly dampen the quilt top with a spray of water. Wipe with a soft cloth to remove any beads of water, then paint the dye solution along all the quilting lines. Apply enough "dye" so it can bleed into the adjacent areas. Use as much or as little as pleases you, remembering that the color will be slightly lighter when dry. Allow to dry thoroughly to dissipate the slight coffee aroma that penetrates the batting.

With a nonbleeding fabric marker, add your name, the date, and the recipient's name to the back of the little quilt.

Pattern 1
1¼″ Square

Pattern 2
⅞″ Square

Summer Sails

A CUDDLY CRIB QUILT

FINISHED SIZE: 42 X 50"

*T*he blue and white nursery of a tiny sailor will sparkle when this flotilla of miniature sailboats anchors in the crib. Soft white cotton is the background for dozens of 3" blue gingham sailboats, their sails trimmed with bright yellow, sailing against a summer sky. Fluffy, but light, machine-pieced and machine-quilted, this is a practical quilt for a little one to snuggle into when the bathroom regatta has ended.

Make extra sailboat blocks to make several pillows—one for the crib and one for the rocking chair. Stitch three blocks together in a row, make a white border, and frame them as a small picture to carry out a nautical theme. Add a bit more color if you like by using blue piping and a blue backing instead of the white pictured.

(continued)

Materials

- ☐ **White cotton muslin, 44" wide: 4 yards**
- ☐ **Light blue cotton for sky: ¼ yard**
- ☐ **Blue check cotton for boat: ⅛ yard**
- ☐ **Dark blue cotton for water: 12 x 12"**
- ☐ **Bright yellow cotton for sail trim: 12 x 12"**
- ☐ **Deep maroon cotton for mast: 12 x 12"**
- ☐ **50-weight cotton mercerized thread: white for hand quilting**
- ☐ **60-weight cotton mercerized thread: white for machine quilting**
- ☐ **Cable cord: 5½ yards**
- ☐ **Low loft quilt batting: crib-size package or 43 x 51"**

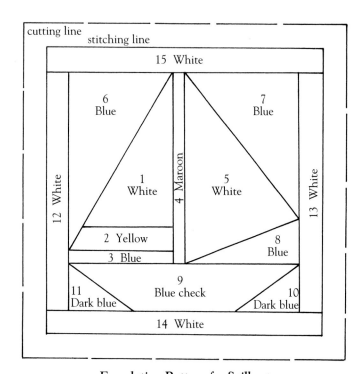

Foundation Pattern for Sailboat

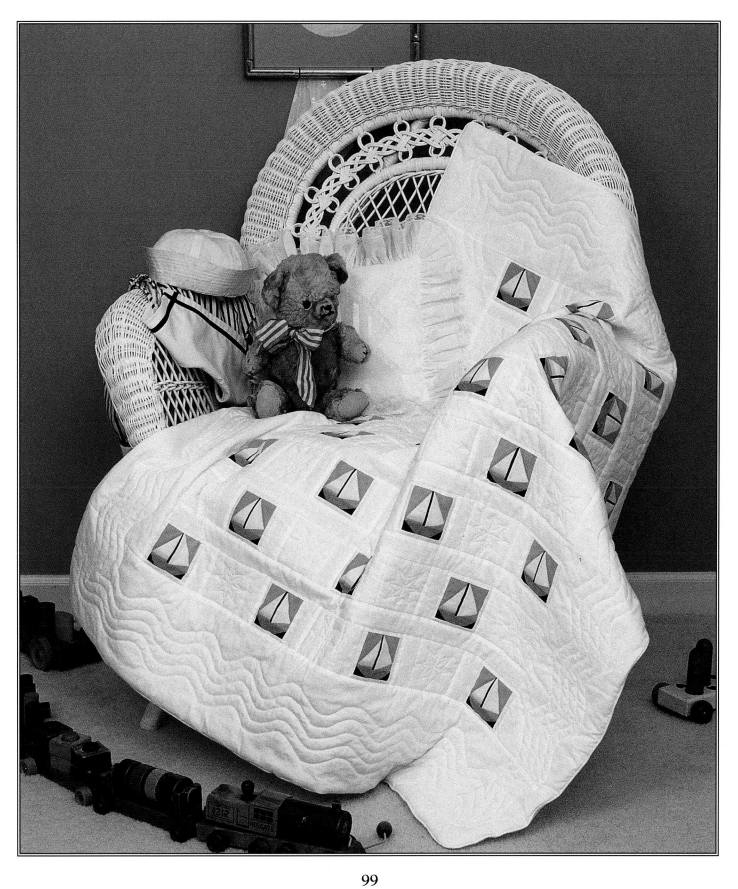

(continued)

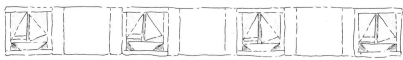

Figure 1

Cutting Guide

☐ **From the white muslin cut:**
the quilt backing, 44 x 52"
2 borders 7½ x 37"
2 borders 7½ x 44"
8 sashing strips 1¾ x 29"
54 sashing strips 1¾ x 3½"
31 squares 3½ x 3½"
Enough 1"-wide bias strips
to total 5½ yards. Use the
remaining pieces for the
sails.

Cut the little pieces for the sailboat blocks as you stitch.

THE SAILBOAT BLOCKS

Copy the *Foundation Pattern for Sailboat* and reproduce it so there are 32 patterns. Using the 50-weight white thread and placing the colors

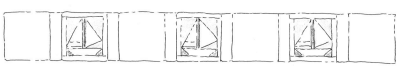

Figure 2

in sequence as noted on the foundation pattern, stitch 32 blocks. Leave the paper in the blocks.

ASSEMBLING THE PIECED FIELD

Stitch together the short sashing strips, the 3½" white squares, and the sailboat blocks to make 9 horizontal strips. Make 5 strips with four boat blocks as shown in *Figure 1*. Make 4 strips containing 3 boat blocks as shown in *Figure 2*. Take care to stitch accurate ¼" seams. As each strip is stitched, press the seams inward toward the sashing strips.

Beginning and ending with a strip like *Figure 1,* join the 9 horizontal rows by alternating them with the

long sashing strips. Trim off any extra length at the ends of the sashing strips. Press all the seams toward the sashing pieces. The piece measures 28¾ x 36¾" and resembles the center field in the color drawing of the quilt.

Remove the paper from the sailboat blocks.

BORDERS

With right sides together and making a ¼" seam, stitch the 7½ x 37" border pieces to the sides of the piece. Trim the ends even with the boat piece. Press the seams toward the border.

With the right sides together and again making a ¼" seam, stitch the two 7½ x 44" borders to the top and bottom of the piece. Trim the ends of the borders if necessary. Press the seams toward the borders.

(continued)

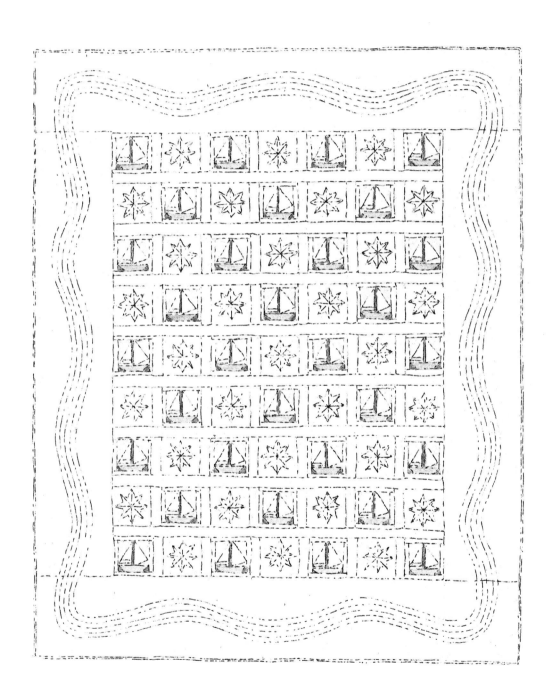

◇

(continued)

Following the instructions on page 153, make 5½ yards of corded piping. Trim the seam allowance of the piping to ¼". Matching the raw edges of the piping and the quilt top, stitch the piping to the entire outside edge of the top.

MARKING FOR QUILTING

Making a line heavy enough to be visible through the white fabric, trace the little **Mariner's Star Quilting Design** and the square enclosing it. Matching the square to the edges of the blocks, trace the star in each white square.

Mark the center of each of the four border pieces. Draw a diagonal at each corner of the border,

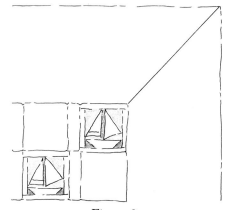

Figure 3

Mariner's Star Quilting Design

beginning at the corner of the sailboat block and ending at the corner of the border as shown in *Figure 3*.

Trace the **Wave Quilting Design** and the slashed line marking the center point.

Placing the slashed line marking the center of the wave quilting design at the center of the border, trace the the design from the center to the diagonal line at the corner. Trace all the way to the diagonal as shown in *Figure 4*.

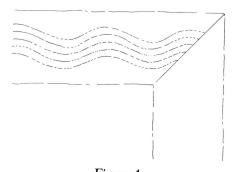

Figure 4

Begin again at the center and trace to the diagonal at the other end of the border.

Repeat for all four sides. The border design will meet in a corner pattern as in *Figure 5*.

(continued)

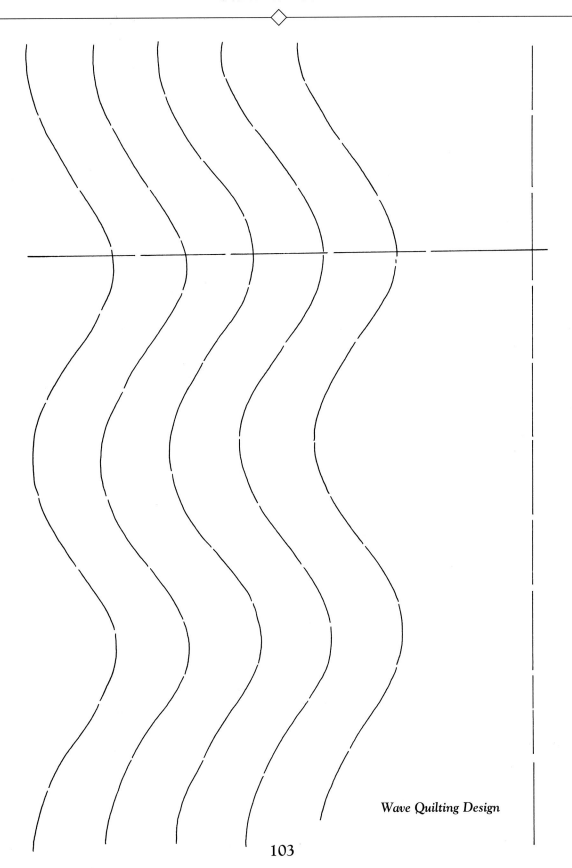

Wave Quilting Design

(continued)

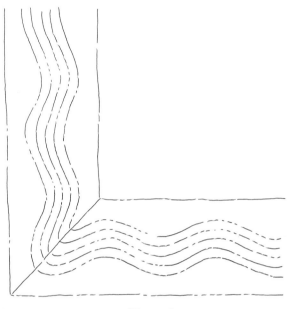

Figure 5

QUILTING

Lay the quilt backing on a large flat surface wrong side up. Place the batting on top and smooth out any extra fullness or wrinkles. Place the pieced quilt top on the batting. Pin the layers together securely. If the quilting is to be worked by hand, baste the three together, placing the basting rows about 2" apart. Machine quilting can be stitched with only the pins.

For machine quilting use 60-weight cotton mercerized thread in bobbin and on top and a stitch length of 2.5-mm. For hand quilting use 50-weight cotton mercerized thread.

Begin quilting by stitching "in the ditch" along both sides of the eight horizontal sashing strips. Then stitch around the entire pieced field. This stabilizes the quilt and allows most of the pins to be removed.

Stitch the wave border designs next.

Stitch "in the ditch" on both sides of the 3" sashing strips.

Finish by stitching the mariner's stars. These can be quilted with a minimum number of threads to be tied if you begin by stitching the four connecting lines from point to point, then continue around the outside instead of cutting the thread at the end of the last line.

Pull thread ends through to the back of the quilt, thread them into a needle, and bury them in the batting.

FINISHING

Trim the batting and the backing to the same size as the quilt top. Turn the raw edges to the inside along the piping and stitch in place by hand.

Add your signature and the little sailboat label described in Special Touches on page 160.

Precious Charmer

◇

A MINIATURE QUILT FOR A LITTLE BED

(continued)

◇

(continued)

Played with by children, grandchildren, nieces, and friends over a period of about forty-five years, the little mahogany bed had lost its canopy, original bedspread, and mattress. It looked forlorn, but the last little granddaughter loved it and still tucked her dolls under its makeshift covers when she visited. It clearly was time to refurbish the cherished little charmer.

A bit of wax cleaned its original finish, but left it intact in case the first owner might become a collector someday. A lace-edged dust ruffle and a new mattress of quilt batting covered with muslin were the next step. The old pillow was wrapped in a piece of batting and covered with white muslin to protect it. Then a lace-trimmed antique handkerchief was used to make a bolster cover.

Finally, it has a new quilt antiqued to look as if it might have been made when the bed was new. The individual squares are just ½ x ½". Tiny, but possible with the foundation piecing method. Cut from dozens of pastel, natural, and white fabrics, that have been dipped in a coffee solution described on page 158 to age them and to balance the colors. The quilt does not contain batting and is not quilted— that would have made it too bulky—but the seams joining the tiny patches create a quilted look. It was fun to make and fairly quick since there is no pattern to follow.

This bed is small. It is part of a well-known line of wood furniture produced in the fifties for 8" dolls. For a scale reference, it is shown with a Madame Alexander 8" Prince Charles doll from the same era. Your bed will probably be a different size and shape, so specific instructions for the quilt as far as size and exact quantities of materials are not given. This is one of those wonderful projects that can come right out of the scrap bag.

(continued)

Materials

- ☐ **A collection of small cotton prints, white cotton, and ecru cotton in pieces as small as 1x1", but preferably about 1x6" for ease in handling**
- ☐ **Plain cotton muslin or a small print for the backing**
- ☐ **Plain cotton muslin for the 1"-wide borders**
- ☐ **60-weight cotton mercerized thread to match**
- ☐ **Fine-point fabric pen with brown ink**
- ☐ **Fabric markers in pink and green**

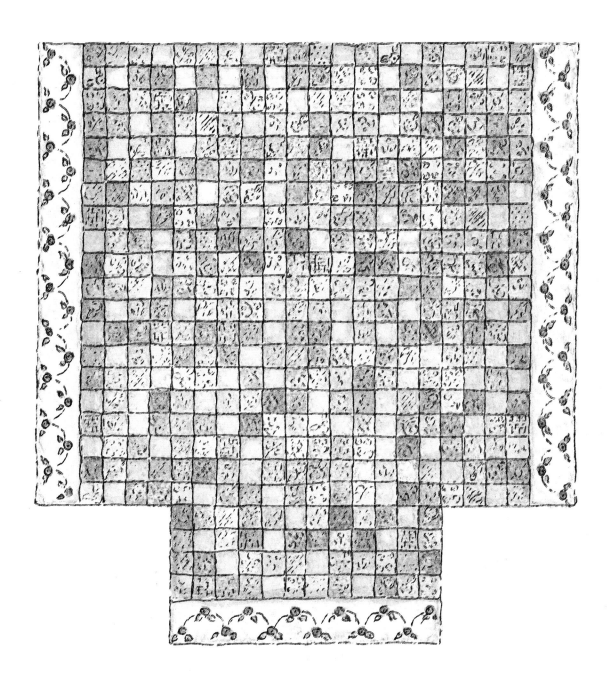

◇

(continued)

To begin, measure the width of the bed. Decide the depth of the drop at the sides and add to determine the finished width of the quilt.

Repeat to determine the length of the quilt. (This bed is a reproduction of a poster bed, for which quilts must be made with a cutout at the lower corners for the posts. The instructions are for a traditional rectangular quilt. If your bed is a poster, simply make the pieced top with a square-shaped area left out at each corner at the foot end as in *Figure 1* and the color drawing.)

Deduct 1" borders from the totals to determine the size of the pieced section. Use ¼" seam allowances in your calculations.

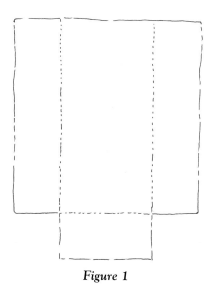

Figure 1

Copy the **Foundation Pattern for Precious Charmer,** repeating the ½" squares as many times as needed to obtain the width. End with the ¼"

seam allowance as on the partial pattern given. Make as many copies of the pattern as you will need to complete the length. (Multiply length by 2 to find the number needed.)

Cut an assortment of 1"-wide pieces. These can vary in length depending on how much of each you wish to use.

Beginning at one end of a strip, and selecting the pieces at random, stitch together the series of squares. Stitch along the cutting line as suggested in the **Foundation Piecing** directions on page 155. Then carefully trim the paper and fabric to make the long strips. Make as many as you need.

Carefully working on the stitching lines of the paper, stitch together the strips to make the pieced top. Press the seams open and do not trim them. (They give the quilt its quilted look.)

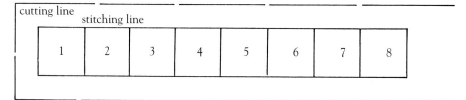

Add as many ½" increments as needed to complete the width of the quilt.
End with the ¼" seam allowance.

Foundation Pattern for Precious Charmer

Remove the paper backing pieces.

Cut the muslin edge strips 1½" wide. Stitch them to the pieced top, making a ¼" seam. Press well.

You can either trace the **Floral Vine Pattern** or draw it freehand. (To draw the pattern, see the instructions below.) Trace the pattern and transfer the design onto the muslin borders before you attach the backing.

Using the completed top as a pattern, cut a backing to fit.

With right sides together and leaving part of the seam across the top open for turning, stitch the backing to the top in a ¼" seam.

Turn right side out. Close the seam at the top. Press.

Using the **Floral Vine Pattern** and the brown fine-point pen, draw the floral vine across the muslin borders. I like these touches drawn freely, feeling that is a more accurate

antique look, but if you would rather trace them, do it before the backing has been sewn on so you can see through the fabric.

Using the pink and green fabric markers, color the flowers pink, the leaves green. Leave the vines brown.

If you wish, antique the piece using the coffee "dye" described on page 158.

Finish furnishing your bed to suit yourself or your favorite little girl.

Floral Vine Pattern

Blue Canton

◇

The Pineapple pattern is one of the very old quilt designs that was always stitched on a foundation. Although it is an easy one to love, it never enjoyed the strong devotion the Log Cabin pattern did, even though it is no more difficult to piece and can be set in as many interesting ways. It is a delightful design in a monochromatic scheme as in the borders of this place mat, but just as pretty in contrasting or print fabrics.

The reduced geometrics of the antique Pineapple pattern stitched in colors to match favorite china make a gracious setting for casual or formal meals. The padding of the traditional-weight batting is protection for a fine table or unexpected luxury for a picnic. The pattern adapts easily for either a small luncheon-size mat or a more generous dinner-size mat. It could also be lengthened to make a runner if needed. Buy extra yardage of one of the blues to make napkins or use crisp white linen ones. Your special quilting as a background will add to the enjoyment of a gourmet meal or just a simple cup of tea. *(continued)*

Materials for One Place Mat

- ☐ **White-on-white cotton print, 42" wide: ½ yard**
- ☐ **Navy abstract cotton print: 9x9"**
- ☐ **Navy cotton solid (#5): 1 quilter's quarter**
- ☐ **Light blue cotton (#1), medium blue cotton (#2), medium dark blue cotton (#3): ⅛ yard each**
- ☐ **Dark blue cotton (#4): 10x10"**
- ☐ **Classic or traditional batting: luncheon size 11x16", dinner size 13x17½"**
- ☐ **Cord for piping: 1¾ yards**
- ☐ **50-weight blue cotton mercerized thread for piecing**
- ☐ **60-weight white cotton mercerized thread for construction and quilting**

Cutting Guide

- ☐ **From the white-on-white print cut:**
  the backing: for the luncheon size 12x16" for dinner size 14x19"
  1 piece for center section of the mat: for luncheon size 10½ x5¼" for dinner size 12¾ x7¾"
  Enough 1"-wide bias strips to total 1¾ yard
- ☐ **From the navy abstract print cut 1x1" squares: 16 for the luncheon size, 20 for dinner size**

Cut the small strips of blues and white as you stitch.

(continued)

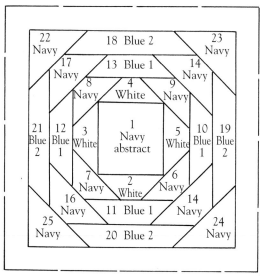

Foundation Pattern for Small Pineapple Block

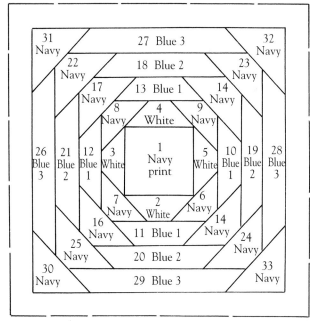

Foundation Pattern for Large Pineapple Block

MAKING THE BLOCKS

BLOCKS ARE 2¼ X 2¼"
AND 2¾ X 2¾"

Trace the **Foundation Pattern for Small Pineapple Block**. Copy to make 12 patterns for the luncheon size (or 16 for the dinner size). In the following instructions, numbers for the dinner-size place mat are given in parentheses.

Stitch in the numbered sequence to make 12 (16) blocks. Use the 1" navy abstract print squares as the center pieces #1. After the four white sections the shades of blue have been numbered 1 to 5 indicating shades of intensity from light to dark, with 1 being the lightest. Use the shades in that order.

Trace the **Foundation Pattern for Large Pineapple Block** and copy it so there are 4 patterns.

Following the numbered stitching sequence, placing the shades of blue in the same manner and adding the dark blue #3 to the last row, make 4 blocks.

(continued)

(*continued*)

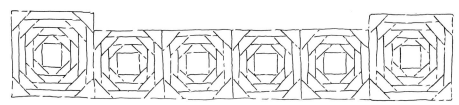

Figure 2

ASSEMBLING THE PIECED TOP

Make ¼" seams throughout. For the smaller place mat stitch 2 small blocks together (3 blocks for the dinner size). Stitch 2 (3) more together. Press the seams open.

Seam the joined blocks to the short ends of the white center section to make a piece that looks like **Figure 1**. Press the seams toward the blocks. All drawings show the luncheon size. Construction is the same for the dinner size except for the number of blocks used.

Stitch 4 (5) small blocks together in a horizontal strip. Sew a large block to each end of the strip, keeping one edge straight as shown in **Figure 2**. Make 1 more piece exactly the same. Press the seams open.

With right sides together, seam the straight side of one strip to each side of the piece. Press the seam toward the blocks. The piece will look like

the color drawing at this point (except that the quilting is not done yet).

Using the pieced top as a pattern, cut the backing piece and the batting to fit the top.

Remove the paper from the blocks.

Draw a horizontal and a vertical line through the center white section to divide it into quarters.

Copy the **Quilting Design for Center Section** including the long slashed lines. Matching the slashed lines to the lines on the center section, trace the first quarter of the quilting design onto the white section. Still matching the slashed lines to those on the drawing, rotate the paper to trace the other three quarters of the design.

Figure 1

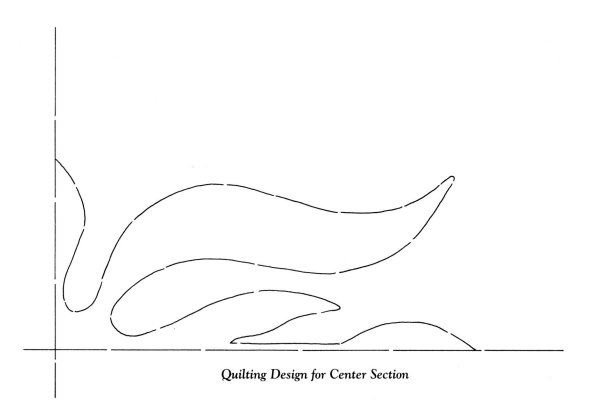

Quilting Design for Center Section

ASSEMBLING THE PLACE MAT

Following the instructions on page 153, make 1¾ yards of corded piping using the 1"-wide bias strips. Trim the seam allowance of the piping to ¼".

Matching the raw edges of the piping to the raw edges of the pieced top, stitch the piping to the outside edge of the top. Clip at the corners so the piping will lie flat.

Place the backing on a flat surface, wrong side up. Follow with the batting and the pieced top, right side up. Pin the three together carefully.

The quilting design is a continuous one prepared for easy machine quilting, but would be equally pretty stitched by hand.

Using whichever method you prefer and the white thread, quilt the pattern in the center section and "in the ditch" around the white section. Tie the ends and bury them in the batting.

Turn the raw edges of the backing and the pieced top to the inside and fasten with invisible stitches.

115

Festival

◆

Sprightly Tulips Signal an End to Winter

Finished size: 9¾ x 14" exclusive of the frame and mat

*I*t takes eight tiny pieces of fabric sewn into a 2" square to make a tulip. Almost an impossible task without foundation piecing, which adds a new dimension to miniature patchwork. What fun this is! Not much investment in time or money, but the result is a picture-perfect little quilt to frame and enjoy for years. Vivid pastel colors and this very contemporary patchwork design make this little piece everyone's favorite.

Purchase a standard-size frame in a style you like and have a mat custom-cut in a shade of pink that matches the tulips and the pink border fabric.

(continued)

Materials

- ☐ White cotton, 42" wide: ⅛ yard
- ☐ Green cotton print for leaves and stem: 12 x 12"
- ☐ Solid pastel cottons for flowers, pink, blue, lavender, and yellow: 8 x 8" each
- ☐ Print pastel cottons for flower centers, pink, blue, lavender, and yellow: 6 x 6" each
- ☐ Black-background floral cotton print: 1 quilter's quarter
- ☐ Allover pink cotton print: 1 quilter's quarter
- ☐ Cotton muslin for backing: 15 x 19"
- ☐ Traditional quilt batting: 11 x 15"
- ☐ 60-weight cotton mercerized thread: off-white
- ☐ Transparent nylon quilting thread
- ☐ Picture mat with 9¾ x 14" opening
- ☐ Picture frame
- ☐ Small amount instant bonding glue

Cutting Guide

- ☐ From the black floral print cut:
  - 2 strips 1 x 18"
  - 5 strips 1 x 3½"
  - 4 strips 1 x 2½"
  - 2 strips 1½ x 13"
  - 2 strips 1½ x 10½"
- ☐ From the allover pink print cut:
  - 2 pieces 2½ x 9⅛"
  - 2 pieces 2½ x 3½"

Cut the small pieces for the patchwork as you stitch.

(continued)

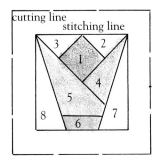
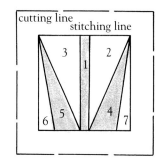

Foundation Patterns for Small Tulip Blocks

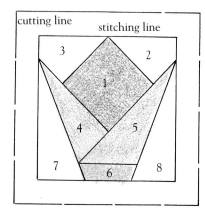
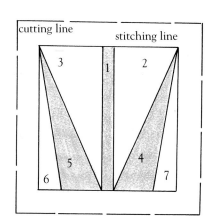

Foundation Patterns for Large Tulip Blocks

MAKING THE TULIP BLOCKS

LARGE TULIP BLOCK IS
1½ x 1½"
SMALL TULIP BLOCK IS
1 x 1"

Trace the 2 *Foundation Patterns for Small Tulip Blocks* and 2 *Foundation Patterns for Large Tulip Blocks*. Copy so there are 4 each of the 1½" large tulip blocks for the center panel and 8 each of the smaller 1" blocks for the border.

Stitch the larger blocks first. Make 1 tulip flower of each color (pink, blue, yellow, and lavender), placing the print as shown by the darker color on the foundation pattern and stitching in the numbered order. Be very careful to finger-press the pieces flat so the points of the petals and leaves will be perfect.

Make 4 stem and leaf sections following the numbered stitching order.

Repeat to make 8 small tulips—2 pink, 2 blue, 2 yellow, and 2 lavender—and 8 stem and leaf sections.

(continued)

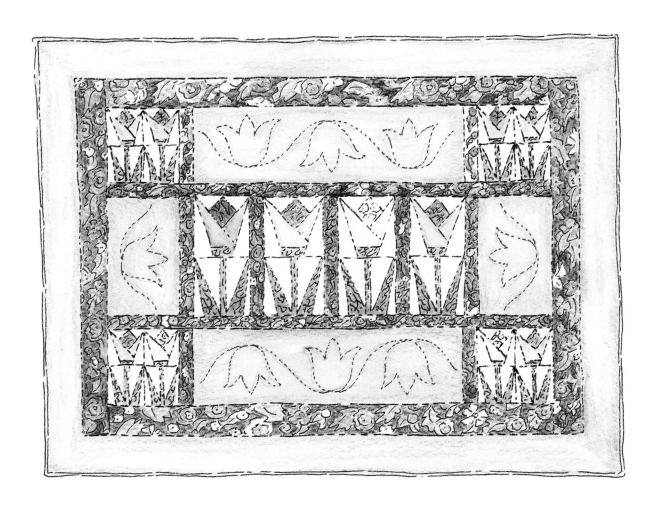

Matching the seam allowances on the paper, stitch the appropriate stem and leaf section to a flower section. Press the seam open.

CENTER PANEL

Beginning and ending with a 1 x 3½" black floral strip and arranging the tulips as shown in **Figure 1**, stitch the four large tulips together. Stitch the strips to the tulips with the paper on top so the stitching line is visible to make stitching an exact ¼" seam easy. Do not trim the seams. Press them toward the black print. (The seam allowances on the tulip blocks are shown as very small dots in **Figure 1** and the black print sashing strips are shown as gray.)

With right sides together, seam a 2½ x 3½" pink print piece to each end of the panel. (These pink pieces are shown at each end of **Figure 1** detached from the tulip strip.) Press the seams toward the black.

Stitch a 1 x 18" black print sashing strip to the top and bottom edges of the panel. Press the seams toward the black.

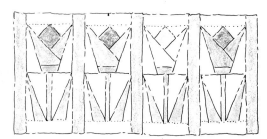

Figure 1

Figure 2

BORDERS

With right sides together, stitch the small tulips together in pairs. Arrange the pairs as in the color drawing of the quilt. Two pairs are pink and lavender and two are blue and yellow. One blue and yellow pair is arranged so the yellow is on the left; in the other, it is on the right. The pink and lavender pairs should be joined the same way. Press the seams open.

Stitch the four 1 x 2½" black print strips to the small tulip blocks, attaching one to the yellow tulip side on the blue and yellow blocks and one to the lavender side on the pink and lavender blocks. Press the seams toward the black.

Stitch the black print sides of the blue and yellow blocks to the 2½" ends of a 2½ x 9⅛" pink print piece. Press the seams toward the black. Repeat with the pink and lavender blocks. One of the border strips now looks like **Figure 2**. The other is the same except that the tulips are pink and lavender.

Stitch the border piece with the pink and lavender tulips to the top of the center panel, checking to

center

Tulip Quilting Design

make sure the black lattice strips line up. Press the seam toward the black print. Repeat with the other border piece at the bottom.

OUTSIDE BORDER

Stitch the two 1½ x 13" black print strips to the top and bottom edges of the piece. Press the seams toward the black.

Stitch the two 1½ x 10½" black print strips to the sides of the piece. Press the seam as before.

Remove the paper foundations.

QUILTING

Copy the *Tulip Quilting Design* including the outside lines and the slashed line marked center.

Measure the pink border sections and mark all four with a line denoting the center of the long sides. Match the center line of the quilting design to the center line on one long border and align the outside design lines with the edges of the panel. Trace that portion of the quilting design onto the panel. Turn the paper over and trace the other half of the design. Repeat for the

other long panel. Note that the center tulip points in toward the center panel.

On the shorter side panels, trace just 1 tulip (which points toward the center) and as much of the stem line as is needed.

Lay the muslin backing on a flat surface. Center the batting on it, then center the quilt top on the batting. (Both batting and muslin are larger than the quilt top.)

Pin the layers together. With the nylon thread on top and the cotton thread in the bobbin, machine-quilt "in the ditch" on all the seam lines except those inside the tulip blocks. Pull the threads to the back, leave 1" and clip.

With the off-white cotton thread, hand-quilt the tulip design in the borders. Sponge out any markings.

ASSEMBLING THE PICTURE

Center the quilted piece over the cardboard back for the frame. Gently pull the muslin to the back and glue to the cardboard.

Check the mat to make certain that ¼" of the black print border will extend under it on all sides. Trim the batting so it is ¼" smaller than the quilted piece on all sides to keep its bulk from extending under the mat.

Using just a touch of glue along the edges, glue the black print to the muslin.

Insert the mat and the picture into the frame and secure with small brads.

Festival Miniature

◇

SPRINGTIME TULIPS TO FRAME

FRAME OPENING IS 4½ X 6"; FRAME IS 8 X 10"

*P*ut the garden catalog away long enough to stitch together six little blocks, vivid floral prints, soft pastels, and a 4x6" piece of batting to make a bright little picture that brings spring's first tulips indoors. The tulips are the same ones that are in the center panel of the Festival picture (page 117), but they could be used in a number of other ways. Two tulips would make a block for a sampler quilt, the top section of the lower blocks would make good lattice blocks, a tulip quilt would be a sweet addition to a little girl's room, pillows would be fun to make.

The three flowers in this little picture are all blue to accent the blue inner mat. They could be three colors as in the Festival picture. Have a bit of fun with this while you wait for the delivery service to arrive with your plants.

MAKING THE BLOCKS

Trace the **Foundation Patterns for the Large Tulip Blocks** on page 118 and copy so there are 3 flower and 3 leaf and stem sections.

Following the numbered sequence on the foundations, stitch all the blocks using the blue floral print for the flower centers, the solid blue for the long petals, and the black floral print for the stems and leaves. Use the white-on-white print for the background.

Join the flower blocks to the stem and leaf blocks in a ¼" seam. Press the seams open.

Join the three tulips into one piece. Press the seams open.

THE BORDER

These border pieces are cut wide to extend under the mat and be glued to the back of the cardboard backing. Stitch the two 3½"-long pieces to the ends of the tulip piece. Press the seam toward the black.

Stitch the remaining two pieces to the top and bottom of the piece. Press the seam toward the black.

Remove the paper from the tulip blocks.

(continued)

Materials

- ☐ **Black cotton floral print:**
  1 quilter's quarter
- ☐ **Blue cotton floral print:**
  1 x 3"
- ☐ **Blue cotton solid: 6x6"**
- ☐ **White-on-white overall**
  cotton print: 10x10"
- ☐ **Traditional quilt batting:**
  4x6"
- ☐ **60-weight cotton mercerized**
  thread: off-white
- ☐ **Double picture mat with**
  smallest opening 4x6"
- ☐ **Picture frame: 8x10"**
- ☐ **Small amount instant**
  bonding glue

Cutting Guide

- ☐ **From the black floral print,**
  cut:
  2 pieces 4x12"
  2 pieces 3½ x 4"
  Cut the small pieces as you work.

(continued)

ASSEMBLY

Place the batting under the tulip panel, centering it. Baste it in place.

Center the panel and batting on the cardboard backing of the frame. Check position by placing the mat over it. Gently pull the raw edges to the back side, leaving the batting loose enough to be softly puffy. Glue the raw edges down.

Insert mat and picture into the frame and fasten with small brads.

Jeweled Star

$\diamond$

A CALICO STAR TO FRAME

FRAMED SIZE: 5 X 5"

*T*he beautiful Mariner's Star quilt pattern is one that almost every quilter dreams of using. Intricate and requiring perfect piecing to achieve its true glory, it is also the one that displays the quilter's art to best advantage. It is a pattern that has historical ties, yet adapts easily to contemporary settings and usage.

One block, reduced to miniature size and pieced using the foundation stitching method, makes a handsome desk accessory when framed in a ready-to-use purchased frame. Jewel-

(continued)

Materials

- ☐ **Light gold cotton with small print: 1 fat eighth**
- ☐ **Small cotton prints in dark gold, dark red, light red, dark blue, light blue: 8 x 8" of each**
- ☐ **Ecru-on-ecru print: 10 x 10"**
- ☐ **Traditional quilt batting: 5 x 5"**
- ☐ **Gold frame with 5" opening**
- ☐ **60-weight cotton mercerized thread: off-white**
- ☐ **60-weight cotton mercerized thread: gold**
- ☐ **Small amount instant bonding glue**

Cutting Guide

- ☐ **From the light gold cotton print, cut a 7 x 7" square for the mat**

Cut the other small pieces as you stitch.

like colors of red, blue, and gold lend a deep richness to the design, but the same gem-toned feeling could be worked out in other colors to fit the color scheme of another room setting.

Four blocks stitched together in a square, the edges piped in silken cord with tassels, would make a spectacular pillow to star in a masculine den. The block edged with sashing strips would make a beautiful addition to a sampler quilt.

MAKING THE BLOCK

Making the block requires that 8 sections be stitched, then combined into the star. Trace the **Foundation Pattern for Star Sections** and copy the tracing to make 8 foundations.

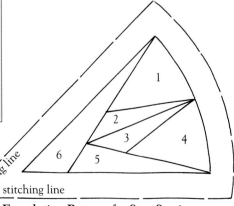

Foundation Pattern for Star Sections

Figure 1 illustrates one-quarter of the block. The diagonal line divides the quarter into the two sections that make up the quarter. The color arrangement for the sections is noted. Working so the right side of your foundation pattern is on top, make 4 pieces like Section 1 stitching the colors noted in the numbered order.

With the foundation patterns turned over so you are working on the wrong side, make 4 sections placing the colors as noted on Section 2 of *Figure 1.*

With right sides together and alternating the sections, stitch the eight pieces into the star-centered circle. Trim each seam to ⅛" and press it open as you progress.

Fold the 7" square of light gold print into quarters and press to mark the sections.

With a compass using the 2" radius shown in *Figure 1,* draw a circle centered on the gold square. (Trace the circle from Figure 1 if you do not have a compass handy.)

Using off-white thread and a 1.5-mm length straight stitch, machine-stitch on the circle outline to reinforce it.

Trim out the center of the circle leaving a ¼" seam allowance inside the stitching line. Clip the seam allowance at regular intervals around the circle. Cut to the stitching, but not through it.

Turn the seam allowance to the inside and press well.

Place the mat with its circular opening over the star. Make certain that the red points of the star intersect the mat at the fold lines marking the sections. Pin and baste the two together.

With tiny hand stitches and gold or off-white thread appliqué the mat to the star piece. Press.

FRAMING

Use the cardboard back in the picture frame as the base on which to mount the star. Touch it with glue in several places and lay the batting on it.

Center the block over the batting and pull the raw edges to the back. Glue the edges to the cardboard. Insert into the frame. Do not use the glass provided with the frame.

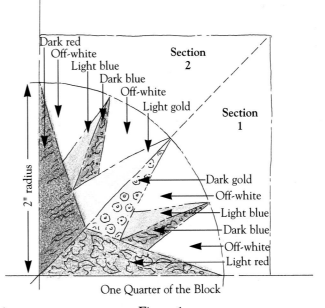

Figure 1

Little Beauty

◇

A DELICATE STENCILED BEAUTY

FINISHED SIZE: 32 X 32"

Delicate appliqué designs similar to those found on the fabled Baltimore Bride and Album quilts can be reduced in size and stenciled in pale pink and green on white batiste to make a softly sweet hanging with lovely scalloped edges. To actually stitch these small designs is possible, but stenciling is a wonderful way to recreate them.

Although these are adaptations of favorite old appliqué designs, each has a new element added—a circle ties the crossed tulips together, the president's wreath is embellished with a curved diamond—to give the piece a contemporary feel. The border is an adaptation of one of the rose blocks placed to accent the scalloped edge.

This design could be enlarged to make a crib quilt by repeating the blocks or by using a copier to change the size of the blocks from 5" to 6". Appliqué enthusiasts might want to stitch the 6"-blocks rather than stencil them.

LAYOUT

Wash both the pink and the white 36" squares to remove the sizing. Iron dry. Set the pink batiste aside for use as the quilt backing.

Place the white square flat on a table to mark the layout grid. Use the **Layout Drawing** on page 130 as reference and mark as follows.

Materials
- ☐ **White batiste, 42" wide, 100% cotton: 1¼ yard**
- ☐ **Pink batiste, 42" wide, 100% cotton: 1 yard**
- ☐ **Stencil film: ten 9x17" sheets**
- ☐ **Stencil paint or cream for fabric or stencil crayons: pink, green, and pale gold**
- ☐ **60-weight cotton mercerized thread: white for construction**
- ☐ **50-weight cotton mercerized thread: white for quilting**
- ☐ **Traditional quilt batting: 36x36"**
- ☐ **Cord for piping: 5 yards**

Measure down from the top edge 1" and draw Line 1 across the piece.

From Line 1, measure down 6" and draw Line 2, which is 20" long and centered.

Draw blocks 1, 2, 3, and 4. All blocks are 5" square.

Extend the lines outlining Block 1 downward to mark Blocks 5, 6, and 4.

Using the same measurements, finish marking the blocks outlining the 10" center square.

(continued)

Cutting Guide
- ☐ **From the white batiste, cut one 36x36" square then, cut enough 1"-wide bias strips to total 5 yards**
- ☐ **From the pink batiste, cut one 36x36" square**

For optimal accuracy, cut the two 36" squares on a pulled thread.

(continued)

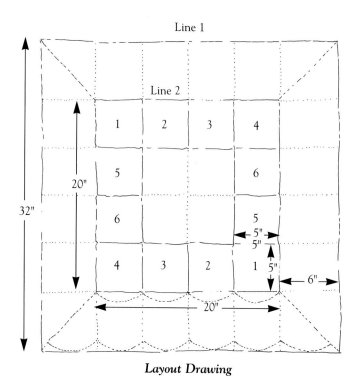

Line 1

Line 2

1   2   3   4

5   6

20"

6   5

5"
5"

4   3   2   1   5"

32"

6"

20"

Layout Drawing

STENCILING

Following the instructions on pages 164 and 165, use the drawings for the blocks, scallop, center, and border sections to cut one stencil for each color shown. One-fourth of each block is shown and is all of the design necessary to cut. Draw the outline of the 5" square on each stencil, then match the outline to the lines on the batiste to correctly place the designs.

Although two shades of pink are shown on the Stencil Designs, only one shade of paint should be used. Cut a stencil for each shade of pink. Use the same paint for both stencils. Apply the paint to the first stencil shading it more heavily at the edges. When paint is applied to the second stencil, the two will be separated by a sharp line.

Before applying stencil paint, check to make sure it will not go over any marking. Once painted over, the mark will be permanent and will show through the transparent paint. If you have used a

(continued)

Measure out from the 5" blocks and mark a 6" border on the other three sides. Draw the diagonal lines to the corners.

Extend the lines defining the blocks to divide the large center square into quarters as shown by the dotted lines. Extend the lines to the outside of the border as shown by the dotted lines on the **Layout Drawing.**

From the **Stencil Design for Border** (page 137) and the **Stencil Design for Border Corner** (page 136), make a tracing of the scallop edge. Place this under the fabric so the deepest point of the scallop is on the outside line as shown on one edge of the Layout Drawing and trace the scallops. One scallop should fit into each 5" section and the end of the scallop for the corner should just reach the diagonal line.

Stencil Design for Center Square

wash-out pen to lay out the grid, just dab the mark with a damp cloth to remove the marks.

THE CENTER SQUARE

The long slashed lines through the drawing of the *Stencil Design for Center Square* match the dotted lines on the center square on the batiste. On the stencil film copy the portions shown on the design and extend the lines so they are all 5" in length measuring out from the center point. When the stencil is correctly centered, the lines will match the lines on the fabric.

Trace and cut out just as much of the design as shown. Color this portion, clean the stencil, turn it over, and color the remaining portion.

Cut one stencil for the areas shown as green and yellow. Cut a stencil for each of the two shades of pink.

THE BLOCKS

Cut one stencil for each color shown on the stencil designs. On the

(continued)

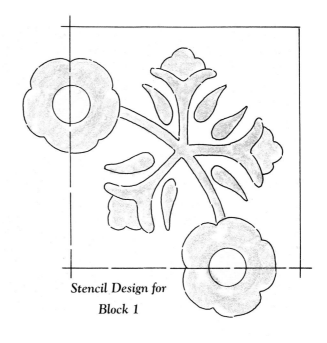

Stencil Design for Block 1

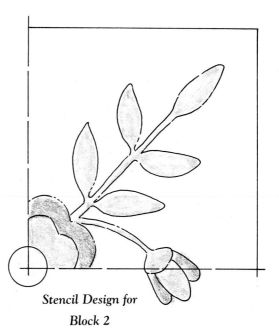

Stencil Design for Block 2

Stencil Design for Block 3

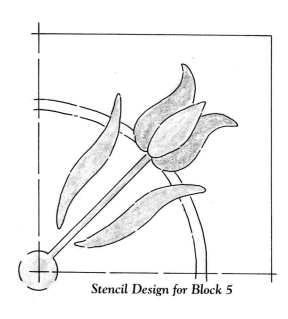

Stencil Design for Block 5

Stencil Design for Block 4

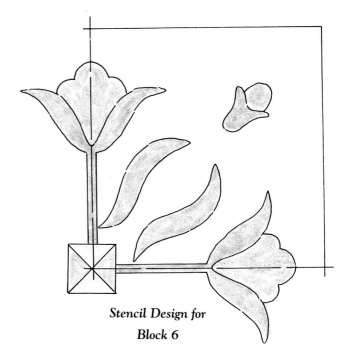

Stencil Design for
Block 6

stencil film copy both the slashed lines dividing the blocks into quarters and the outside line defining the 5" block. Match the outline to the lines on the quilt top and use the slashed lines as aids in placing the designs.

It is necessary to cut only the one fourth of the design shown. Rotate the stencil to color the complete block.

The blocks are numbered to facilitate distribution. Match the number on the block to those shown on the Layout Drawing.

THE PINK SCALLOPS

Cut a stencil for one scallop from the *Pink Scallop Stencil Design.* Place the straight edge of the scallop stencil on the edge of the blocks as shown by the dotted line on the Layout Drawing. Shade the scallops by working more color into the edges than in the center. Paint 16 scallops, one at each block edge.

THE BORDER

Make a tracing of the *Stencil Design for Border* and the *Stencil Design for Border Corner.* They join at the

(continued)

Block 1
Apply paint lightly for a soft pastel effect

Sample Stencil

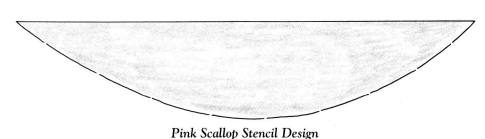

Pink Scallop Stencil Design

(continued)

long slashed line. Make one stencil for the green and yellow sections. Make another stencil for the portions of design shown as pink. Trace the scallop line on the stencil.

Place the stencil so the scallop line on the stencil matches the one drawn on the batiste. Move to repeat. At the corners paint the half

on which the stencil fits. Finish the rest of the border. Clean the stencil film and turn it over to finish the other half of the corners.

ASSEMBLING THE QUILT

Stitch the 1" white bias strips into one continuous piece and follow the instructions on page 153 to construct 4½ yards of bias piping. Trim the seam allowance of the piping to exactly ¼".

Trim the quilt top to the scallop shape, allowing a ¼" seam allowance beyond the scallop line.

Matching the raw edges and clipping the piping as necessary, stitch the piping to the scallops on the outside edge of the quilt top.

Layer the backing, the batting, and the quilt top, smoothing out all

Join border stencils at this line

Stencil Design for Border Corner

wrinkles. Pin and baste, placing the basting rows about 1½" apart.

Hand-quilt using the 50-weight cotton thread. Stitch on all the lines outlining the various sections and around each flower or leaf motif.

Stitch inside each pink scallop, placing the rows ¼" inside the outline. Place another row of stitching outside the scallops, placing this row also ¼" from the pink edge.

Place a row of quilting inside each of the 16 blocks and inside the large center square so it is ¼" from the first row of quilting. All these lines are shown on the color drawing of the quilt.

Sponge out any remaining markings.

Trim the edges of the batting and the backing to match the top.

Turn the raw edges to the inside and fasten with small invisible stitches. It will be necessary to clip the quilt top to the stitching at the top of each scallop. A matching clip will make the backing and batting lie flat at this same point.

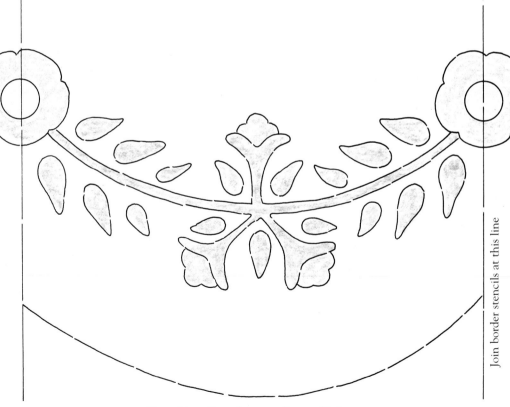

Join border stencils at this line

Place this scallop edge on scallop on fabric

Stencil Design for Border

Materials

Quilters love fabrics; they collect beautiful colors and interesting prints as well as ones that will add a special texture or sparkle to a quilt. The accumulation grows and so does the inspiration it radiates. As we use precious pieces, we save every scrap we think we might use someday. All of us dream of the special charm quilt that will contain all those wonderful pieces. It will be a delightful quilt, large and very intricate in design. Each scrap will be sewn with the tiniest stitches and the memories and the love in our hearts will be made into a thing of beauty that our descendants will treasure. Surely there will be time to start tomorrow!

Tomorrow always arrives on time, bright and sunny and filled with a busy schedule that necessitates putting off designing the quilt for another day. The fabric collection grows, folded neatly in a box or on a shelf. Meanwhile another collection—the scraps—is filling another box, or boxes. Miniature quilts are a wonderful way to put some of those beloved scraps to use, and there might be enough time today to start one. Get out your boxes and think small. In many cases you will not have to buy a thing in order to start!

FABRICS

As for larger quilts, the quality of a miniature is dependent on the quality of the fabrics used in it. While most of the miniatures we make won't be subjected to as much wear as a quilt used as a bedcover, and we aren't designing and making them necessarily to become heirlooms, construction and final results are much finer when the best materials are used. For the most part, 100% cotton fabrics are preferred. They are easier to cut, sew, press, and quilt. In the last few years there has been a veritable explosion of newly designed quilting cottons, each collection more wonderful than the last. The perfect color, print, or texture for most any need is available.

Many of the miniatures included in this book can be cut from your stock of remnants, but it may be necessary to buy pieces large enough for the backing or perhaps just the right print to unite a collection of scraps. If so, look for a smooth finished cotton that is tightly woven so the edges of the tiny pieces won't fray during construction and so the ⅛" seam allowances won't disintegrate in later washings.

Most of the good quilting cottons are 42" to 45" wide. For the purposes of the materials lists with the instructions, the 42" width has been used. If your fabric happens to be the wider width, you may have a bit extra, but not enough to reduce the yardage suggested. When it is necessary that the wider width be purchased (as for a crib quilt), that has been specified so you can be certain of having the right width without seaming.

There has always been a bit of a debate about whether we should wash quilting fabrics before use. Some say, "Absolutely" if the fabric is going to shrink or bleed, it will do so in the prewash rather than in the finished masterpiece. Other quilters like to test small swatches and then work with the crisp new fabrics. The decision is personal, but it really is a convenience to start stitching with a collection of prewashed fabrics, neatly ironed and stacked by color, waiting for a creative moment.

It is not necessary to put the fabrics through a full cycle in the washing machine. Just wet the fabrics, agitate a moment, rinse, and iron to dry. If the fabric loses its body, a small amount of spray starch will restore the original finish. Tiny pieces of fabric are easier to cut and handle if they have a bit of body.

Iron dark colors on a white towel. If one is going to bleed, you'll identify it immediately.

Many of the miniature quilts are constructed using an old foundation piecing method that was largely reserved for Log Cabin, Pineapple, and crazy quilt patterns. Expanded now and developed for these tiny quilts, the method also makes it possible to use a wide range of fabrics usually ignored by quilters because they are so difficult to cut and sew. This technique allows the use of a bit of metallic glow or the gleam of silk or satin in a little quilt. All manner of other fibers and textures can be used creatively since the backing stabilizes them. If you use a selection of fragile fabrics, take care that all materials can be treated in the same manner for washing or dry cleaning and check for colorfastness.

The natural first impulse when selecting fabric for a miniature quilt project is to limit the choices to the myriad tiny prints available. They are wonderful, many being reproductions of vintage patterns and colors, but large-scale prints are also beautiful and useful. Choose big prints for color and texture, knowing that the entire repeat will probably never be used. They can become the most valuable pieces in a design. A beautiful scrolling print in shades of gray or dark brown with feathers drawn in a finely etched black line

(continued)

(continued)

can be cut for tree trunks or the roof of a little house, yielding a beautiful natural look that is much prettier than a patch of solid brown or gray.

Large floral and pictorial prints cut into miniature pieces often yield similar results. Overall abstract prints that at first seem too modern for a traditional quilt are sometimes just the right spark to bring a design to life. Collect quilter's quarters of some of these in colors and patterns you like. You'll find yourself using them in many ways.

Neutral white and natural-colored cottons used to be the mainstay background colors to be kept on hand for lattice strips, plain blocks, background pieces, and backing. Add to that staple list the same colors embellished with all manner of patterns that match the background. These add a richness and depth that belies their simplicity. Both white-on-white and ecru-on-ecru are basics that should be part of your collection.

Quilt shops and mail-order suppliers sell their fabrics by the yard, with an eighth of a yard usually being the minimum cut they will make. They usually also have a collection of their best sellers cut into "quilter's" or "fat" quarters. These are half-yard cuts, divided in half so the resulting piece is 18 x 22", often a more economical measurement than 9 x 42". Some suppliers also sell fat eighths for the same reason.

Another delightful way to buy little samples of lots of prints or solids is to purchase fabric packets. These are usually 4", 5", or 6" die-cut squares of a selected range of colors or prints. One might be all blues, reds, greens, or pastels in a wide range of prints. Another may be a collection of solids in rainbow or pastel colors. A package of one hundred squares would probably contain two squares each of fifty different prints. Packets are fun and a big help when choosing colors for miniatures. Most of the fabrics are also available by the yard, so it is possible to buy larger quantities for sashing and backing.

BATTING

As with full-size quilts, the batting has almost as much effect on the final appearance of the quilt as do the fabrics. There is a wide array of quilt battings available today. Fibers can be cotton, silk, wool, and polyester. Loft ranges from very low to very high. For the tiny quilts, very little loft is needed. Sometimes nothing is needed! The materials list for each quilt tells you exactly what was used in the pictured quilt.

Some battings are less bulky, allowing the tiny stitches of yesterday to be made, while others are thick and fluffy. Some will shrink just a bit to suggest that the quilt is old; some are warmer than others. The loft of the quilt batting is indicated by the names the manufacturers call their products. For miniatures, low-loft, classic, and traditional fleece are the most frequently used. In the materials list for each quilt, batting is noted by these names. The packaged battings bearing these names are usually polyester with a coating on the outside of a fluffed inner mass. The coating holds the batting together and prevents the fibers from migrating. Even a miniature quilt, which presumably will not be as heavily used as a bed-size quilt, will benefit from the use of the best-quality batting.

The small size of the miniature dictates that batting not be too fluffy. Too much loft and too much quilting will make a stiff miniature. If the lighter weights noted in the materials list are not available, consider pulling a thicker batting apart to make one more suited to the little quilt. Many use cotton flannel, which adds just a bit of fluff, as a substitute for batting. Some pieces, like the little Precious Charmer on page 105, rely on the bulk of the seam allowances to give just enough texture to a miniature.

THREAD

Thread seems a trivial detail, but it is actually very important because it can make a pleasant or a difficult project, an enduring treasure or a disappointment. If it snarls or breaks frequently, the piecing and quilting are onerous tasks rather than fun ones. If it is not strong enough, the seams come apart or the quilting stitches break. If it is stronger than the fabric, it will cut the fabric—too heavy and it will ruin the effect of little stitches.

For best results use only 100% cotton mercerized thread for both piecing and quilting. Mercerization is a chemical process that makes thread strong and smooth, thus good for hand or machine sewing. Cotton is best for use on cotton fabrics because when pressed, its stitches flatten and seem to become part of the fabric rather than remaining a row of little loops sitting on top of the fabric as do polyester and blended fiber threads.

Fine-gauge threads have been used for construction of many of the little quilts in this book since these are mostly decorative, and the fine thread does facilitate accurate piecing. For hand quilting, 50- and 60-weight cotton thread are excellent for these little quilts. Although they are appropriate for larger projects, most of the waxed cotton quilting threads are a bit to heavy to be pretty on the little quilts.

For machine quilting on the miniatures, 50- and 60-weight cotton threads are very good. Machine-quilting threads with a matte finish are very good for larger quilts and can be used if necessary for machine work on the miniatures. For stitches that do not show except for the indentations they make, try a transparent nylon thread that is easy to use and very strong. Fine and soft, this thread is available in both clear and smoke. It can be used both on the top and in the bobbin, or just on the top with cotton in the bobbin.

For construction, match the color of the thread to the colors of the work as well as possible. For light colors, white or off-white thread is generally good. Decide which is dominant when working with a mixture of light and dark. Often the best solution is off-white or beige which really matches neither, but does not contrast greatly either. For hand-appliqué stitches, match the thread color to the appliqué color.

Basic Sewing and Quilting Supplies

SEWING MACHINES

Although they are exciting and efficient, modern, state-of-the-art, computer-controlled sewing machines are not required for quilting. If your machine makes a good straight stitch and the tension is adjustable, you are ready to begin stitching. One necessity that you may have to add—whether your machine is new or old—is a walking or dual-feed presser foot. This is a device that replaces the utility presser foot and helps feed the top layer of the quilt at the same rate the feed dogs move the lower layer through. Without it you will almost always end with a little pleat at the end of the stitching no matter how carefully you baste or pin. One of the best-known machines has this device built in. Others have a special presser foot—called either a walking foot or a dual-feed foot—that does the job.

If there is not a specific dual-feed or walking foot made for your machine, take the machine to a dealer to be fitted with an adapter that will make it possible to use one of the newer versions of these presser feet. There are now all kinds of generic attachments that make sewing easier.

On the other hand, if you own one of the new computer-controlled sewing machines, your appreciation for all its conveniences will grow when you begin quilting with it!

For the best machine piecing, good tension, pretty, straight stitches, and a clean, well-maintained machine are the most important considerations. Keep a can of air by the machine and blow the lint and dust out of the bobbin compartment and the feed dogs every time you sit down to sew or fill the bobbin. This will prevent accumulated lint from being stitched into your quilt, leaving a gray mess that is sometimes very difficult to pick out.

Change the machine needle often, even if it seems to be stitching perfectly. About eight hours of sewing is enough for most needles.

Stitching through both fabric and paper, as is done on most of these little quilts, causes a bit more wear on the needle than conventional stitching on just fabric.

SCISSORS AND CUTTING TOOLS

Construction of a quilt requires two basic pairs of sharp, well-cared-for scissors. A good pair of 8" or 9" shears is necessary for cutting fabric, batting, bias strips, etc. A small pair of embroidery or utility scissors is handy for trimming and for snipping thread ends.

For foundation piecing, in which one often cuts through layers of both fabric and paper, it is a good idea to buy a pair of inexpensive plastic-handled steel scissors and keep them by the machine. Usually made in the Orient and kept at the front of the fabric store as an impulse item, these are surprisingly good and save your expensive dressmaker shears, which should never be used for paper.

A rotary cutter, mat, and special ruler are other good investments. They can save many hours of tedious work marking and cutting fabrics. For making these small quilts, look for a mat about 18 x 22", a small cutter, and a clear plastic ruler with a lip at one end.

PINS AND NEEDLES

Glass-headed pins that are a little longer and quite a bit sharper than standard straight pins are a necessity when pinning together the layers of a quilt. You'll like them so much they will replace the old pins for traditional sewing as well as quilting.

Keep a supply of sewing machine needles on hand. For piecing, construction, and machine quilting on these little pieces, a size 80 needle is good. As noted previously, change it after about 8 hours of sewing. This is particularly important when the foundation piecing method is used. The paper makes the development of little burrs or rough spots that can cut thread more likely.

For hand quilting, the best needle is the one with which you are most comfortable. Many quilters use a needle called a "between" or "quilting" needle. It is a short needle with a round eye. The shorter length supposedly makes it easier to rock back and forth to gather stitches on it. A size 11 is average, but you might prefer a larger size 10 or a smaller size 12. Buy a package of assorted sizes and select the size that is best for you.

A size 9 or 10 crewel needle can also be used for hand quilting. This is a tapered needle a bit longer than the between. It has an elongated eye that is easy to thread and is preferred by many quilters because its tapered shape makes it easy to pull through the layers of a quilt.

PRESSING EQUIPMENT

For most sewers a good iron is almost as important as a good sewing machine and that is especially true of quilters. Each seam should be pressed and trimmed after it is sewn,

(continued)

(continued)

and for work with cottons, it is best if the iron has adjustable heat settings and makes enough steam to do a good job. Most household irons meet these requirements and are all that is needed.

A well-padded ironing board is also essential. A cover marked into 1" grids — available at retail stores— is a big help for lining up pieces and seams.

MARKING TOOLS

Of all the tasks needed to put together a beautiful project, most quilters like marking the top for quilting the least. Miniatures need very little quilting, and since a lot of it is outline quilting and stitching "in the ditch," very little marking is entailed.

Since much of the marking for these little quilts is in the borders and can be rinsed out easily, you will probably find a wash-out pen or pencil the preferred marker. The pens make lines that are easily followed, but it is a good idea to test

any marker before using it on a quilt. Simply mark on a piece of the fabric used for the quilt, then rinse it to determine if the markings will really wash away. Iron the piece dry to see if the marks come back; if they do, be certain they can be washed away permanently.

Most of the blue wash-out markers do disappear when dabbed with water. If the marks should reappear, rinse the piece with cold water, allowing the water to flush out the chemicals. Do not add soap or detergent to the water. They turn some marks brown and make others permanent.

Instead of drawing lines, make a series of dots. Always try to mark the quilt top before it has been assembled with the batting and backing to prevent any ink from seeping into the batting.

For signing your quilts, use a fine-point fabric pen with permanent ink. For coloring little areas like the border on the doll quilt on page 105, use markers created specifically for fabric. These will not bleed and are usually permanent.

PAPER FOR FOUNDATION PATTERNS

The instructions for the quilts stitched with the foundation piecing method tell you to copy the foundation pattern and make a number of copies of it. The best paper for both the original tracing and the copies is lightweight parchment tracing paper. Buy a pad of the 9 x 12" size in an art supply store and cut it to 8½ x 11" for the copier. See page 154 for important tips about using the copier to reproduce these patterns.

The Basics of Miniature Quiltmaking

If you enjoy sewing but have put off making a quilt because it seemed so daunting a project, the miniature could be the beginning of a lifelong odyssey into quiltmaking. Miniatures are fun because they are small and quickly completed, yet they incorporate within their little borders most of the skills needed for a traditional quilt.

MINIATURE VOCABULARY

These terms apply to both miniature and traditional quiltmaking.

Appliqué. A decorative stitching technique used to attach a fabric decoration to another fabric.

Backing. The fabric used for the back or undecorated side of a quilt. Sometimes referred to as the lining.

Basting. Long temporary stitches used to hold pieces together during construction.

Batting. The fluffy inner layer of a quilt; it adds warmth and loft.

Bearding. The migration of batting fibers through the outside fabric of a quilt.

Bias. Fabric cut at a 45-degree angle to the selvages to maximize stretch and drape.

Binding. A narrow strip of fabric—usually bias—used to finish the edges of a quilt.

Block. One unit of a quilt design.

Fat quarter. A method of dividing a yard of fabric into four squares measuring 18x22", allowing best use of the small piece. Also called a quilter's quarter.

Field. The pieced or ornamented top without the borders.

Foundation pattern. A paper or fabric pattern onto which the pieces of a patchwork design are stitched. The paper is usually removed after stitching has been completed, while the fabric remains as part of the quilt.

Grain. The horizontal and vertical threads of the fabric.

Lattice block. The square that is used to connect lattice strips when two colors are used.

Lattice strips. Narrow strips of fabric used to join the blocks of a quilt top.

Loft. The degree of thickness of batting.

Miter. A method of joining corners at 45-degree angles, similar to a picture frame.

Piecing. Stitching together small pieces of fabric to make a patchwork design.

Quilter's quarter. The same quarter yard cut as a fat quarter.

Quilting. The stitching that holds the three layers of a quilt together, while at the same time adding decoration and texture.

Sashing. Another term for lattice strips.

Set. The way in which the decorative blocks of a quilt top are assembled.

Stitching "in the ditch". The placement of a row of stitching in the groove of a seam line.

(continued)

Template. A piece of plastic, cardboard, or paper used as a guide for tracing quilting designs or for cutting patchwork pieces.

Whipstitch. A small, invisible hand-sewing stitch used to finish the edges of a quilt.

GETTING STARTED

If quilting is a new experience for you or if you want to venture into the world of miniatures, begin by reading through the brief descriptions of materials and equipment on the preceding pages. Although short, they tell you the most basic requirements for making miniature quilts. Most sewers already have most of the tools and materials needed to start. Add a few new quilter's quarters for inspiration and a pad of parchment paper, dig out your collection of scraps, and you are ready to stitch!

Review the Foundation Piecing instructions on page 154 and make several copies of the **Basket Weave Foundation Pattern** that is used as an instruction tool there. Also copy some of the block patterns from other quilts that look interesting to you. Stitch these to check your sewing machine and seam allowances as well as to see if you are going to enjoy this miniature work. Some of us become addicted to it— we love the precision and the speed!

Next, try a block from one of the little quilts that was made by a more traditional, but still fast, piecing method which does not utilize the paper foundation. Memories (page 92) which is a greatly reduced version of the old favorite Bow Tie pattern, and the equally diminutive Pastel Bear Paws (page 48) are both fun to piece.

Finally, stitch several crazy quilt blocks like those used for the Victoria Christmas stocking (page 56). Notice how small shifts in the placement of the patches change the overall design. Wouldn't it be fun to hang stockings like this next Christmas?

You are ready!

FABRIC PREPARATION AND CUTTING

After the selected fabrics have been washed, ironed, and tested for colorfastness, they should be trimmed to a straight edge. This can be done by placing a ruler across the fabric at a right angle to the selvage and cutting it with a rotary cutter, by pulling a thread and cutting on the line left by the removed thread, or by tearing across the fabric.

When the last method is used, the edge is very straight and exactly on the grain, but the edges curl slightly and must be pressed. Those annoying loose threads must also be cut away. Pulling a thread is time-consuming, but a very accurate method. When the rotary cutter is used, the cut edge may be several threads off-grain in some spots, but the cut is so sharp and straight that this is seldom a problem. Rotary cutting is the fastest method as the edges are uniformly clean-cut and several layers of fabric can be cut at once.

Since precision cutting is one of the keys to accurate quiltmaking, you will find that you use all three methods depending on the project— tearing long pieces for borders and sashing, rotary-cutting small pieces and strips, and pulling threads on delicate fabrics.

In several of the quilts, the instructions include patterns for some pieces as well as instructions for cutting the same pieces with a rotary cutter. Use the method you find fastest and most accurate. If you use the patterns, carefully trace them on stencil film or cardboard to make templates. Cut the templates out, then draw around them on the fabric. Draw carefully so the point of the pencil stays as close as possible to the edge of the template to avoid making pieces that are larger than intended. Always line up straight edges of the templates with the vertical or horizontal grain of the fabric.

The Cutting Guide that precedes the instructions for each quilt is important even if you do not intend to start by cutting all the little pieces you will need before beginning to stitch. Check it and always cut the large pieces first to ensure that there will be enough fabric to cut them without piecing.

You will notice that the Cutting Guide often suggests that the little pieces needed for foundation piecing be cut as you stitch. That is part of the fun of that method. Usually it is best to have a strip of each color by the machine to be snipped as it is needed. Be sure to cut the pieces large enough to include the seam allowances. After you have stitched the sample block in the Foundation Piecing instructions—in which the pieces have been measured for you—you will feel secure about this wonderfully easy way to cut the tiny pieces.

STITCHING SEAMS

For work on miniature quilts, make a habit of stitching $\frac{1}{4}$" seams unless another width is specified. In most cases these seam allowances should be trimmed to $\frac{1}{8}$" after pressing. Check your machine. Many have been designed so that when the right edge of the basic or utility presser foot runs along the raw edge and the needle is in its central position, it will make a line of straight stitches exactly $\frac{1}{4}$" from the edge. If this measurement is off by only a thread or two, the finished pieced area will not measure correctly.

To make certain your seam is an accurate $\frac{1}{4}$", make a test sample by stitching two pieces of fabric together in a $\frac{1}{4}$" seam. Measure from the cut edge to the stitching. Check carefully—about $\frac{1}{4}$" is not good enough! If you need to make an adjustment and your machine has variable needle positions, try moving the needle. If not, place a piece of tape on the throat plate to mark a line along which to feed the pieces. With foundation piecing this is not a problem in the blocks because all you do is stitch on the lines on the paper. However, you will need the accuracy for assembling the quilt.

PRESSING SEAMS

Press each seam as it is stitched. Using the steam iron and the setting for the material being used, press the

(continued)

(continued)

seam flat. Trim the seam to $\frac{1}{8}$". Then press the seam toward the darker of the fabrics unless the instructions specify pressing differently.

When using the foundation piecing method, it is not necessary to press every seam. Simply finger-press neatly as you turn the pieces to the right side and hold them in place until the next piece has been stitched—another bonus in this quick piecing method!

MARKING FOR QUILTING

There is very little marking needed for the quilting on these tiny quilts. In fact, there is very little quilting! Read the Materials section (page 138) for advice about markers and then follow the specific marking instructions in the quilt directions.

After the quilting has been completed, remove all traces of the markings. The markings of most wash-out pens and pencils—which are very good for such tiny projects—can be sponged out. If the marks come back after the piece is dry, rinse them out by holding the quilt under a stream of water.

PUTTING THE LAYERS TOGETHER

When the top has been pieced, pressed, and marked for quilting, the three layers that make the quilt are layered together and either pinned or basted for quilting. For a little quilt, this is a quick job.

If the pictured quilt has been finished with bias piping, make the piping following the instructions on page 153. Trim the raw edges of the piping to exactly $\frac{1}{4}$". Matching raw edges, stitch the piping to the outside edges of the quilt top with a $\frac{1}{4}$" seam. Allow extra fullness at the corners so the piping rounds the corners nicely.

Place the quilt backing on a flat surface wrong side up. Place the batting on top of the backing, smoothing it so there is no extra fullness. (The batting and backing are always a bit bigger than the finished top. Trim them when directed to in the instructions.) Next, center the quilt top on the batting, right side up.

Pin the layers together. For machine quilting, pinning is sufficient. For hand quilting, add the extra step of basting in rows about an inch apart to keep the layers stable during the stitching.

QUILTING

Miniature quilts require very little quilting partly because of their size, but also because quilting seems to make them very stiff and flat. The stitching can be done either by hand or by machine, or can be a combination of the two. The combination usually consists of machine stitching "in the ditch" around the blocks and lattice strips and pretty hand quilting in the borders where is shows to best advantage. This gives the luxurious look of a hand-quilted piece with very little work.

The instructions for each quilt specify where quilting should be placed, and if a quilting design is needed, it is included with the quilt instructions. For machine quilting it is best if these designs are a continuous line, as are those of the Blue Canton placemat (page 110) and the tulips for Festival (page 116). These require only four thread ends to be tied and buried in the batting. Designs intended for hand quilting—like the star for Summer Sails (page 98)—can be used for machine quilting, but they do entail tying off a greater number of threads. Since machine stitching is so much faster than hand stitching, the little time needed to tie the thread ends is usually not a problem.

Hand Quilting

As noted in the Materials section, the needle and thread are very important components of successful hand quilting. Experiment with different sizes and types of both until you are satisfied that you have found the best for you. Think also about using a thimble. I do not use one, as my pricked fingers attest, but many quilters consider a thimble a basic part of any hand stitching, and it can be helpful if you like to gather four or five stitches on the needle before pulling the thread through. The little dimples on the top of the thimble are not just ornamentation. They help support the needle while you push it through the fabric layers.

If you have never hand-quilted, begin stitching in one of the least conspicuous portions of the quilt or practice on a little sample made of leftovers of the materials in the three layers of the quilt. Follow the stitch instructions, relax, and enjoy the stitching. Although the quilting stitch is the same simple running stitch used for hand sewing, it does take a bit of practice to make it small and even when working through three layers of fabric and batting—it's not difficult, just different in the way it is made and feels.

The prettiest stitches are small and the same size on top of the quilt as on the back. Many quilters feel even size is more important than tiny size. You'll find that your stitches become more regular and smaller as you stitch.

There are three entirely correct methods to achieve pretty stitching. The first is a method quilters and embroiderers call "stick and stab," in which the needle is inserted down from the top and pulled through, then reinserted from the bottom to come out again at the top. This is slow and usually not very accurate, because one has to guess where to insert the needle when it is under the quilt. The second method is worked from the top, using the underneath hand as a help to gather three or four stitches on the needle before pulling the needle through. The most even stitching is done one stitch at a time with one hand on the top, the other underneath guiding the needle. The index finger of the underneath hand can become irritated from being pricked by the needle, but can be protected with a little piece of tape or a plastic quilter's thimble.

(continued)

◇

(continued)

The key to making a pretty stitch is to insert the needle downward through the layers in a straight path as shown in **Figure 1a**. The hand above the quilt top holds the needle between the thumb and third finger

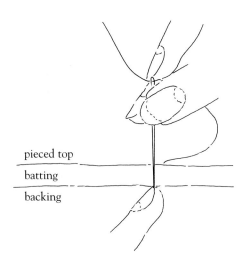

pieced top
batting
backing

Figure 1a

while the index finger pushes the needle down and through the layers until it just touches the tip of the index finger below.

When the finger underneath feels the tip of the needle, it pushes up slightly while the index finger of the hand on top pivots the needle downward until it lies on the surface of the quilt and the tip comes

through to the top *(Figure 1b)*. The thread is then pulled through and the next stitch begun.

Figure 1b

With this method and a little practice, the stitches will become very even and good speed can be developed. If you prefer to gather three or four stitches on the needle and can keep them even, use this same method, pulling the thread through when the full number of stitches has been picked up on the needle.

In the beginning, aim to make six or seven stitches per inch—counting only the stitches on the top. After a bit of practice, the count will be eight or nine stitches per inch. This is very pretty and a perfect size for most quilts.

There will be times when the "stick and stab" method is the only one that will work. These times are

usually when stitching across a seam line or when trying to navigate tight corners.

Stitch with an even tension, pulling the thread just enough to make the stitches lie flat on the surface, making a slightly indented line. Stitches pulled too tightly will break when a quilt is handled or stress is put on them.

Begin and end all threads with a tiny knot buried in the layers. Start with a little knot in the end of the thread. Take the thread down from the top into the batting about ½" from where you want to start stitching, and bring the needle to the top at that point. When the knot reaches the surface of the quilt top at the point at which the needle went in, give the thread a little tug or stroke it with your fingernail until it pops through to the inside. If it leaves a little opening still visible in the fabric, close it by pushing the threads together with the tip of the needle.

End a thread when there are still about 3" in length left in the needle. Use the needle to tie a little loop knot in the thread, and pull the knot down until it is about one stitch length from the surface of the quilt. Insert the needle at the point at which the next stitch would begin, but go down only into the batting and come to the surface about ½" away. Pull the knot through to the inside and cut off the thread end close to the surface. The end will disappear into the quilt.

While large quilts are usually laced into a quilting frame to keep the layers from shifting during this stitching, these small quilts can be quilted easily in hand. New quilters find that this is sometimes a big help while they are learning to improve their stitches. It also means the little quilts travel well to fill in moments that would otherwise be wasted.

Machine Quilting

Although it has been done for many years, machine quilting has not until recently been accepted by quilters as a way to finish a quilt. However, the limits on our time, the new machines, dual-feed presser feet, and

new threads have prompted us to experiment with it. Several well-known quilters have really elevated machine quilting to an art and have developed new techniques that are both beautiful and intriguing. New quilting designs created for the machine consist of continuous lines, which means there are few threads to tie off, making the stitching fun, fast, and durable.

There is very little quilting on these miniature quilts, but many of them have been machine-quilted. Others have been finished with a combination of hand and machine quilting, which lends the luxurious look of hand stitching to the quilt where it is visible and the speed of machine work where stitching simply adds texture.

A miniature quilt that is to be machine-quilted can be secured for stitching with straight pins if they are carefully placed so the layers are held together through the minimal handling the quilt will receive during the stitching. Usually it is enough to pin the quilt in rows about 1½" apart.

Attach or set the dual-feed presser foot, and thread the machine with the thread recommended in the instructions. Use a stitch length of 2.5 mm for these little quilts. Begin stitching in the center of the quilt and work outward. Study the quilt before beginning to decide how to stitch to minimize the number of thread ends there will be to tie off. Do not stitch over pins; remove them as the stitching comes close to them.

After the stitching had been completed, pull the thread ends to the back, tie them, thread them into a needle, and bury them in the quilt batting.

The instructions with each quilt specify the amount of stitching to be done and exactly where it should be placed. It may not seem to be a lot of quilting, but it is enough to enhance the design. Too much quilting placed in rows too close together can make these little quilts very stiff.

(continued)

(continued)

FINISHING THE QUILT

When all the quilting has been completed, trim the layers to the measurements noted in the instructions. When the batting is low-loft, sometimes the finished edge is fluffier if the batting is cut the same as the other two layers. Or, when that would be too bulky, the batting is cut ¼" shorter than the top and backing. Look to the quilt's instructions for advice about this.

There are a number of ways to finish the outside edges of a quilt. Several of these have been used for the miniatures in this book, and instructions for these follow. There are other methods for traditional quilts that could also be used, but these produce a very polished look on a miniature.

Miniature Quilt Edge Finishes

Bias corded piping and binding are two lightweight but elegant finishes for the edges of miniature quilts.

Both are easily applied and not only hold together and finish the edges in a tailored, crisp way but can also be used as an additional decorative element. Bias binding is usually a bit wider than piping, but the two are generally interchangeable.

The fabric for both piping and binding is usually cut on the true bias of the material. This means that the first cut should be made from corner to corner on a square of fabric as shown in **Figure 2**. Subsequent cuts should be made in the width

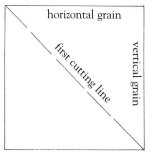

Bias strips should be cut diagonally from corner to corner on a square to obtain a true bias

Figure 2

specified in the instructions and following the line of the first cut. (Some quilters and sewers cut their strips on the straight grain of the fabric and finish their quilts with

perfect edges. Bias, however, is preferable because it is easier to maneuver around sharp corners and scallops. The yardage and cutting guides in the instructions in this book assume that bias will be used.)

To determine the number of strips to be cut, add the total lengths of the four sides of the quilt. Then add another 6" for the corners and ½" for each seam. It is best to routinely add several inches more than will be needed just for security.

Strips cut on the bias have ends that are slanted. To seam these, hold them with right sides together as shown in **Figure 3** and stitch a ¼" seam. Press the seam open. These seams are barely visible after the bias piping or binding have been finished.

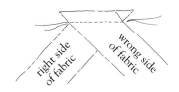

Piecing bias strips

Figure 3

Corded Piping

Piping cord is usually found in the drapery department of fabric stores. It is a soft white twisted cord usually made of polyester fibers. It is available in many different weights ranging from thick ones that are an inch in diameter to tiny stringlike cords. For the miniature quilts look for a thin cord rather like sport-weight knitting yarn. As a matter of fact, cotton knitting yarn in the sport weight is an ideal cord if it is first preshrunk. To do this, wind a length of yarn over a book or other support and tie it in three or four places. Remove the hank from the book and immerse it in very hot water for a few minutes. Hang it to dry, then untie it and wind it into a ball.

To make a piece of corded piping, begin by centering a piece of cord on the strip of bias as shown in **Figure 4a**. With the wrong side of the bias

wrong side of fabric

Figure 4a

up, lay the cord at the center of the strip parallel to the edges. Fold the cord in half as shown in **Figure 4b**. Using a cording presser foot, and

right side of fabric

Figure 4b

holding the cord so it stays against the fold, stitch as close to the cord as possible for the length of the strip. Use a straight stitch with about a 3-mm length.

On an older machine, the zipper foot is sometimes the best foot for stitching close to the cording. A newer machine usually has a cording foot or an edge stitcher that make this job easy. If the machine is equipped with a pin-tuck foot, that is excellent. Allow the cord to run through one groove of the foot and move the needle until the stitching is against the cord. Use the same foot to attach the finished cord to the quilt top.

After the cord has been stitched, trim the seam allowance to ¼" so it

matches the seam allowances on the quilt top. Usually it is best to attach the piping to the edges of the quilt top before the three layers are assembled. Then after the quilting has been completed, the only remaining steps are to trim the batting and the backing, turn the edges to the inside, and whipstitch the backing to the top along the stitching line of the piping.

Bias Binding

Cut and seam as many pieces of bias as necessary to reach around the quilt, adding to the total about 6" extra for turning corners.

After all the quilting has been completed, trim the layers to the seam allowance specified in the instructions. Beginning at the center of the bottom edge of the quilt and with right sides together, stitch the binding to the quilt, allowing enough extra at the corners to make a neat, flat turn.

Press the seam flat and turn the binding to the back. Turn the raw edge under and whipstitch to finish.

(continued)

Foundation Piecing

Some of the favorite traditional quilt patterns traditionally have been pieced on a foundation of either muslin or paper, a method that lends great accuracy to intricate patterns, producing needle-sharp points, square corners, and perfectly matched seams. The Log Cabin group of designs, which includes the Pineapple, Courthouse Steps, the Virginia Reel, and others, is the predominant category, and examples of these date back many years, attesting to the practicality of this piecing method.

The beloved Victorian crazy quilt utilizes a foundation of muslin which remains in the quilt. The muslin adds stability and makes it possible to piece a quilt from a collection of typical Victorian frou-frou that otherwise would be impossible to handle. Heavy velvets, rich silks, and fragile laces can be stitched to one another with minimal problems.

Our interest in miniature quilts has given new meaning to foundation piecing, a technique that makes it possible for us to stitch ever smaller pieces together with the precision we love. It is an easy method that adapts so well to machine piecing that the blocks for a tiny quilt can be made in an afternoon.

If you have never tried foundation piecing but want to try a miniature quilt, stitch the practice blocks in the following section. Try both paper and muslin if you like, but remember that muslin stays in the quilt and is an extra layer through which you must quilt. Paper is a bit tedious to pick out, but a good pair of tweezers makes it a soothing task and these quilts are so small that it is really not enough trouble to be objectionable.

Although it produces very accurate finished results, the foundation method actually makes the precision with which pieces are cut less important than for traditional piecing since the pieces are trimmed to shape after they have been stitched to the foundation. This saves a lot of the preparation time and allows us to begin stitching almost at once.

COPYING THE FOUNDATION PATTERNS

The quilts in this book have been designed and planned assuming you would copy the foundation patterns and work from them, since this is the easiest and most economical method. Purchase a 9 x 12" pad of parchment tracing paper on which to make the copies.

Trace the foundation pattern in the instructions carefully near the center of the paper. (Even the best of copiers distort the image at the edges of the paper, and when you are working with these tiny pieces, a little distortion makes a big difference when it is multiplied across a quilt. If you are careful and keep them as close to the center as possible, two patterns can usually be placed on one page.)

Always working from your original tracing, make as many copies of the foundation as instructed. Leaving about an inch of paper outside the cutting line, trim off most of the extra paper around the patterns.

CUTTING FABRIC FOR FOUNDATION PIECING

Traditionally, when a quilt is started, hours are spent cutting, stacking, and sorting the fabrics for the blocks. With the foundation piecing method there are no templates and no marking. The initial tedium is skipped, and accuracy and fine construction are not compromised.

It is best to cut or tear the strips so they are straight and on grain, but it is not necessary to cut exact little shapes. If you look ahead to the Basket Weave practice piece on page 156, you will note that for each square 4 pieces are needed. Two are $1\frac{1}{8} \times 2\frac{1}{2}$" and 2 are $1 \times 2\frac{1}{2}$". It is easy to cut 2 strips of each width across a quilter's quarter with a rotary cutter. Then stack these by the machine to

cut into $2\frac{1}{2}$" pieces as you need them, since it really doesn't matter if they vary a little bit.

For a first quilt, the exact sizes of all the pieces of the Basket Weave Hanging are specified on page 6. After you have made that—or the practice piece—this method of cutting will seem easy. It is one of the features of the foundation method quilters love best.

STITCHING ON A PAPER FOUNDATION

The seam allowances on these miniature quilts are $\frac{1}{4}$" unless otherwise specified. (Read Stitching Seams on page 147 and adjust your machine if necessary.)

Use a #70 sewing machine needle and the thread specified in the instructions for each quilt. A straight stitch 1.5-mm long is the best for constructing the blocks. Always stitch one or two stitches beyond the ends of the line. With the small stitches and this little overlap, it is not necessary to tie thread ends.

The pieces of each foundation pattern are numbered in the

sequence in which they should be sewn. Follow that order for best results.

Trim each seam to $\frac{1}{8}$" after it is sewn and finger-press the piece flat. It is not necessary to use an iron for every seam with this method.

When all the pieces have been sewn, stitch a final row around the block just inside the cutting line and then trim the block, cutting exactly on the cutting line. Leave the paper in the blocks until the instructions say to remove it. When stitching pieces together, match the edges carefully and stitch on the stitching line for perfect $\frac{1}{4}$" seams.

Basket Weave Block
The little four-piece block that makes the center portion of the bright Basket Weave Hanging is a good one on which to begin stitching. You will need only 4 tiny pieces of fabric and a piece of tracing paper to try this one. From the trial you'll see the accuracy with which your pieces go together and get the feeling of stitching onto the paper foundation.

(continued)

(continued)

◆ Trace the **Foundation Pattern for Basket Weave** onto lightweight parchment tracing paper. Use a ruler and be as accurate as possible. Notice that the stitching lines on the drawing are shown as solid lines, while the outer cutting line is a dotted line. Your pieces of fabric should cover all the way to the edges of the cutting line.

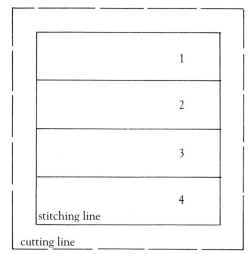

stitching line

cutting line

Foundation Pattern for Basket Weave

◆ Cut 2 strips of fabric 1⅛ x 2½".

◆ Cut 2 strips 1 x 2½". For this little practice exercise, the strips can be all one color or an assortment like the one in the illustrations.

◆ Turn the paper pattern over and place one of the wider strips over the

section marked 1. Place the piece with the wrong side against the paper and line it up as shown in **Figure 1**. The portions of the foundation pattern under the fabric

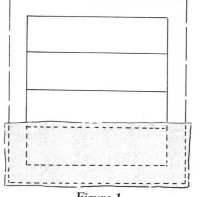

Figure 1

piece are shown as dotted lines. The cut edge of the fabric should extend at least ⅛" above the stitching line. Hold or pin the piece in place.

◆ With right sides together, lay one of the narrow pieces on top of the first piece. Match up the top edges as shown in **Figure 2**.

◆ Holding the pieces in place, turn the foundation over so the paper is on top. Using a 1.5-mm straight stitch, machine-stitch through the layers, placing the stitching exactly on the seam line.

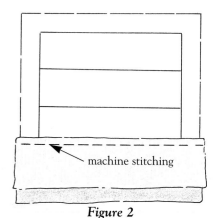

machine stitching

Figure 2

◆ Trim the seam allowance to ⅛" and open the pieces so the top one lies flat as shown in **Figure 3**. Finger-press the seam flat.

Figure 3

◆ Place a third strip (a narrow one) at the top edge of the second one with right sides together as shown in **Figure 4.** Turn the foundation over so the paper is on top and stitch a seam through the layers as shown in **Figure 4**. Trim

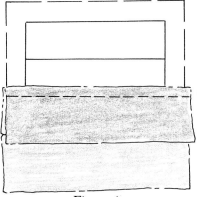

Figure 4

the seam and finger-press the piece flat.

◆ Finish with the other wide strip. The fabric should extend to or slightly beyond the slashed cutting line on the foundation pattern. Finger-press flat.

◆ An optional step which I always take is to stitch around the square, just inside the cutting line. This holds the pieces flat to the edge and makes assembly easier.

◆ Trim through all layers on the cutting line to make a perfect square.

When the blocks are assembled, the carefully cut edges and the marked stitching lines serve as guides, making perfectly joined seams possible. Take advantage of the stability of the construction by not removing the paper foundations until the quilt is partially assembled and the instructions note that the paper should be removed.

PICTURE BLOCK

This block is also called Square Within a Square. It is an easy one to stitch and is especially pretty if a motif from a printed fabric is centered in the diamond, as the teddy bear was in the more complex block used for Barrie's Vest on page 81. Try this block following the numbered stitching order, then try the one for the vest, which builds on this basic unit.

◆ Trace the **Foundation Pattern for Picture Block** onto lightweight parchment tracing paper.

◆ Begin with the center square piece of fabric cut 3x3". Cut a strip of contrasting fabric 1½x10" for the corner pieces. Divide it into 4 equal pieces for the corners.

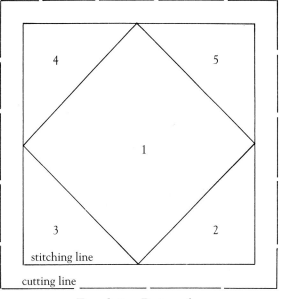

Foundation Pattern for Picture Block

◆ Hold the center square in place and, with right sides together, place the straight edge of piece 2 so the seam allowance is at least ⅛". Hold the piece to the light so you can see where the seam allowance is. Stitch exactly on the line, then finger-press flat. Add the other 3 corner pieces, finger-press them flat, then stitch inside the cutting line and trim the outside edge. Finish the block with sharp points and perfectly straight edges.

Special Touches

───────────────◇───────────────

Your stitching, little changes in design, as well as your choice of fabric and color make these little quilts your own original creations. Other small touches that will endear your work to present-day recipients as well as future generations are embroidery, your signature and recorded historical data, antiquing, and other little things you do automatically. These personal touches tie the quilts forever to you.

ANTIQUING A NEW QUILT

While it is almost impossible to duplicate the patina that the years add to a quilt, it is sometimes possible to create the aura of antiquity by treating fabrics with a dye solution made from coffee or tea. These are fairly permanent dyes, as you know if you have tried to remove a stain made by one of them in a good tablecloth or napkin. Certainly from that experience we know that they will endure the minimal washings a miniature quilt will have in its lifetime.

Antiquing is fun and fast, but not an exact science. You can apply the "dye" after the quilt has been completed, or you can dip all the fabrics to be used into the solution before construction. Often the latter method is used to soften the very bright colors of new fabric.

While either coffee or tea may be used for the dye solution, they produce different shades of brown. Tea tends to have a reddish to orange tint depending on the strength of the solution. Coffee, on the other hand, is usually a deeper, richer brown. To decide which to use, experiment with samples of both on swatches of the fabric to be treated. This process works only on natural fiber fabrics—cotton, linen, and silk. Each takes and retains the dye in its own way.

Making the Dye Solution
Depending upon what you are going to dye, make a pot or a cup of fairly strong coffee or tea. Instant coffee does as well as brewed and is convenient for small projects. Tea

bags are better than loose tea, not because of any difference in the solution but because they don't leave little bits of leaves floating in the dye solution.

If you are going to be treating the fabrics for a quilt, prepare enough coffee or tea in which to submerge the pieces. Use only porcelain or china containers.

Add about ½ cup white vinegar to each quart of coffee or tea.

The Dyeing Process
Wash the fabrics to remove the sizing and rinse well. Do not dry. Roll the fabrics in a towel to remove the excess water, then immerse the wet fabric into the solution to ensure that the dye saturates the fabrics evenly. Boil for about ten minutes, checking the color often. Remember that the color will be a little lighter when the fabrics are dry.

To "antique" a finished quilt, make just a cup of coffee or tea and add the vinegar. Spray the piece with water and fold it for an hour or so until the dampness evens out. Place the piece on an old towel and paint on the dye with a camel hair brush. Apply the dye only to the areas that would have darkened over the years. For instance, on the Memories doll quilt on page 93, dye was painted into all the seam lines, along the quilting of the bow designs in the borders, and in the crease where the ruffle joins the quilt. Touches were added to the embroidery on the eyelet ruffle to give it some age also.

If you use this painted method of dye application, leave the damp piece on the towel to dry so the dye has time to bleed into the adjacent fabric. These pieces are best not placed in a dryer since there is a chance that the heat will set the color before it has a chance to bleed, causing a very patchy look.

Inevitably some of the coffee or tea solution will spread into the quilt batting. This is not a problem, but if coffee has been used, there might be a trace of fragrance left. This dissipates fairly quickly and is not a drawback to the process.

The tiny Precious Charmer quilt on page 105 was also antiqued after it was completed—the entire piece

was just dipped into coffee solution, rinsed, rolled in a towel, then ironed dry. Then a bit of extra dye was painted along the edges of the border pieces to add a bit more age. The result is that the many pastel colors in the diminutive blocks were leveled to a delicate aged look that blends well with the lovely ecru dust ruffle and antique handkerchief used for a pillow sham on the doll bed.

ADDING THE FLOURISH OF YOUR SIGNATURE

The personal touch that only you can add to a quilt is your signature and the date the quilt was made. The notation made in your own script and either penned or embroidered on the back of the quilt will always be a reminder of the love you stitched into the little piece. Don't worry that your writing is not fine enough to be used this way. It is part of you and for that reason will be treasured.

For a miniature quilt the signature should be little—in scale with the

quilt. You will need a very fine pen. Look for one with a 01 point and permanent ink intended for use on fabric. These pens, which come in a number of ink colors, are found in both quilt shops and art supply stores. The ink will not bleed and the fine point allows tiny writing. Ink colors are black, green, brown, red, and blue. Black and brown look the oldest, but any that coordinates with the quilt is acceptable.

A little label stitched to the corner of the quilt is perhaps the easiest way to start. If you don't like it, you can make another. Begin with a piece of washed fabric that matches the quilt. Cut it larger than needed and iron it to the shiny side of a piece of freezer paper. Write directly on the fabric, peel off the paper, trim the label to the size and shape needed, fold under the raw edges, and stitch it to the back of the quilt.

On many antique autograph or album quilts, pretty wreaths or scrolls surrounded the signatures and notations. The variety of these is great and inspires us to create frames

(continued)

159

(continued)

Made for
Meagan Michelle Eastman
by her grandmother
Margaret Boyles
1995

Quilt label adapted from the quilting design for the Memories quilt

for today's signatures. You might want to draw a heart or an oval around yours. Sometimes it is fun to use part of a motif from the quilt as illustrated here with part of the quilting design for the Memories doll quilt on page 93. The foundation pattern for the sailboat block used to make the Summer Sails quilt on page 99 is a personal flourish for that quilt. Stitched to the back of the quilt, it records the year Nikki came into our lives. Barrie's Vest (page 81) has a simple white rectangle sewed to the inside underarm seam that reads, "I love you, Mumsie." She checks that little label before she puts the vest on.

A little label made on a foundation block is appropriate for a miniature quilt pieced that way. Copy the foundation pattern and make one to match the quilt. Begin with a rectangle of muslin 1½x3½". Iron it to the shiny side of freezer paper and write your message on it.

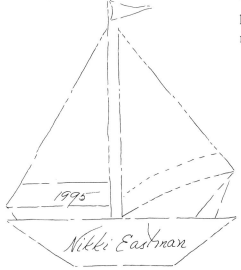

1995
Nikki Eastman

Quilt label adapted from the foundation pattern for the Summer Sails quilt

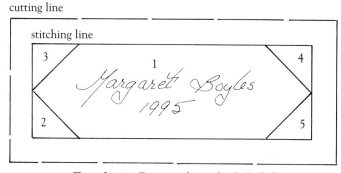

cutting line

stitching line

Margaret Boyles
1995

Foundation Pattern for a Quilt Label

Remove the paper and use the rectangle as the first piece on the pattern, centering your message. Follow the numbered order to complete the block. Turn back the raw edges on the stitching line and stitch the label to your quilt.

You'll have your own ideas for what you write and how you sign your pieces to begin a tradition that will add to the special qualities of every piece you make. Most important, don't omit the date. Time flies!

EMBROIDERY

Like your signature, embroidery is highly personal. Each of us works the stitches using the same instructions, needle, and thread, but the embroidery varies as much as our handwriting does. In addition, we all combine stitches and colors in different ways, adding even more variation. Each finished piece has its own individual beauty.

This unique touch is one that you will want to consider using to make your quilts a gift that could come

only from you. Whether you create a simple outline stitch label with your name and the date for the back of the quilt or indulge in a Victorian pleasure with an embroidery-encrusted crazy quilt, use the basic stitches that follow to enhance your pleasure in miniature quiltmaking.

Experiment with threads spun of different fibers. Six-strand cotton embroidery floss is always beautiful. In addition to coming in hundreds of colors and shades, it is now available in hand-overdyed variations that literally sing with color. Floche, which is slightly heavier than six-strand, is another delightful cotton that stitches up into beautiful satiny embroidery. Pearl cotton is twisted so its beautiful colors stitch into deep textures. Silk is an affordable luxury that adds its royal touch, while linen flower thread makes this wonderful fiber available for embroidery. Silk ribbon is a fabulous addition that opens a whole new world of embroidery. Especially pretty as bits of embellishment on Victorian-inspired crazy quilt pieces, it loops and bends to make a whole

flower with four or five stitches, sometimes a leaf with just a single flat stitch.

For best results, all of the stitches should be worked with a single strand of thread or ribbon. For small stitches use a single strand of six-strand cotton embroidery floss or silk embroidery thread and a size 10 crewel needle. Increase the stitch size by using heavier thread and a larger needle. Floche or pearl cotton in a size 8 crewel needle will yield slightly larger stitches, while ribbon or yarn in a 26 tapestry needle make stitches even more substantial.

Bullion Knot

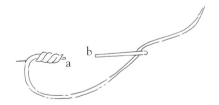

This is a pretty stitch that resembles a rolled coil of thread lying on the fabric. Used often in multiples to make delicate roses, it is also

(continued)

sometimes used for leaves and the petals of other flowers, such as daisies.

To work the stitch, bring the needle up to the surface at **a** and pull the thread through. Go down at **b** and come up again at **a** so the point and about half of the needle shaft are above the fabric, but do not pull the thread through. Wrap the thread around the needle until the length of the coil is roughly the length of the space between **a** and **b**.

Hold the wrap firmly between the thumb and forefinger and gently work the needle until it pulls through the coil. Still holding the coil, pull the thread all the way through so the stitch lies flat on the fabric. Take the needle to the back again at **b**.

If the needle is wrapped so the coil is equal to the distance from **a** to **b**, the stitch will lie straight. To make a curved stitch, wrap several more times.

Feather Stitch

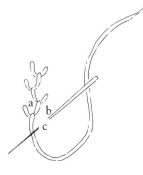

The feather stitch is a graceful vining and trimming stitch. It is a pretty outline for a quilt label and is used extensively as the perfect seam decoration for Victorian crazy quilts.

Begin by bringing the needle to the surface at **a** and pulling the thread through. Lay the thread as shown, insert the needle at **b** and bring it to the surface at **c**. Pull the thread through using just enough tension to make a loop. Reverse direction, making another loop at the other side. Notice how changing the slant of the needle affects the appearance of the stitches. You may want tiny narrow stitches for a vine—wider stitches to cover the seam of a crazy quilt.

Fly Stitch

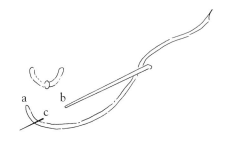

A looped stitch, the fly stitch can be worked as a single stitch or as a continuous chain of the little winged stitches. Another stitch that is lovely on the seams of crazy quilts, it is also attractive worked in ribbon to make quick leaves and flower petals.

Bring the needle to the surface at **a** and lay the thread as shown. Insert the needle at **b** and come up at **c** which is midway between **a** and **b**. Gently pull the thread through with just enough tension to make a graceful loop. Insert the needle on the other side of the thread at **c** and pull through to the wrong side to make the small fastening loop.

French Knot

A single French knot is a pretty accent or flower center, while a solid group adds elegant texture and filling. The most secure knot is wrapped around the needle only once. For a larger knot, use a heavier thread rather than more wraps.

To make the knot, bring the needle to the surface at *a* and pull the thread through. Wrap the thread around the needle once and insert the tip into the fabric close to *a* with at least one thread between the two points. Pull the thread to tighten the loop and bring it close to the surface of the fabric. Pull the needle through to the back of the work.

Lazy Daisy Stitch

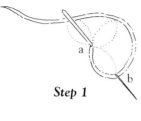

Step 1

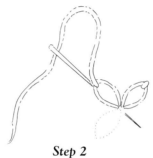

Step 2

Five lazy daisy stitches make a pretty flower; one makes a shapely leaf. Often found on antique embroideries, this is a useful stitch that adds a delicate quality to a design. Quick and easy, it is a favorite of most stitchers.

To begin, bring the needle up at *a* and pull the thread through. Holding the thread below the needle to form a loop as shown in **Step 1**, go down again at *a* and bring the needle to the surface again at *b*. Pull the thread through and adjust the loop. Make a small stitch across the loop to secure it as shown in **Step 2**.

Outline Stitch

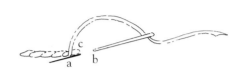

A very useful narrow line can be drawn with the outline stitch. It makes stems or details in leaves, and can be worked solid as a filling or used to outline a filled shape. Care must always be taken to throw the thread to the same side to keep the stitching even.

Begin a line of stitches by bringing the needle to the surface at *a* and pulling the thread through. With the thread above the needle as shown, go down at *b* and come up at *c* exactly halfway between *a* and *b*. Pull the thread through and continue in this manner.

STENCILING ON FABRIC

Stenciling has been a favorite tool of quiltmakers for centuries, and today's new paints, crayons, and creams make it a wonderful way to decorate a quilt top with exuberant color or pattern. Most of the fabrics used for quiltmaking will take and retain the colors well if paints are chosen specifically for the fabrics and the manufacturer's directions for applying and setting the color are followed.

Fabrics to be decorated with stenciling should be washed to remove the sizing. Otherwise the paint will sit on top of the sizing and be washed away when the quilt is washed the first time.

If you haven't stenciled for a long time, look at the new products available. The new paints have a consistency that prevents them from running under the edges of the stencils; crayons and creams are very easy to use and make almost no mess. Stencil film is a weight that cuts neatly and comes in packages or large rolls. A special stencil brush, a good craft knife, and extra blades are usually available right in the stencil department.

Stencil paints are usually acrylic and are formulated for fabric and dry-brush stenciling. They dry quickly and are cleaned up with water. Most of the popular brands are very good.

The stencil crayon is just that—a big fat crayon formulated of linseed oil and pigment in a compressed wax base. It is the most mistake-proof color available. The color is applied to the stencil film around the edges of the cutout opening, then brushed onto the fabric. It makes adding a bit of shading easy, dries overnight, and leaves the fabric as soft as it was originally.

The newer stencil creams are paint that comes in a bit different formula. Packaged in small amounts, they were originally developed for work on clothing, so are perfect for quilts. They are permanent and washable when directions are followed and are produced in a wondrous array of colors.

The stencil brush is a stubby round one with blunt-cut bristles. Buy one for each color you will be using and clean with brush cleaner or soap and water as the manufacturer suggests.

Working on a Miniature Quilt

The piece of stencil film is used not only as the opening through which paint is applied but often as a guide for placement of the design enabling you to avoid making any more marks than necessary on the quilt fabric. If the instructions direct that the outline of a square around a design be traced onto the film in addition to the cutouts for paint, it is so the designs can be accurately placed with the least effort.

In addition, this method of stenciling makes use of several different stencil layers rather than the old bridges to separate colors. Most designs require a stencil for each color unless it is possible to combine two without a problem.

Follow the quilt instructions in this matter. Colored stencil designs make this process easy to understand.

To begin, trace the design on the film with a fine-tipped pen containing ink that will adhere to the film. Draw on the shiny side of the film. Place a cardboard or other mat material under the film and cut out the design. Begin with a new blade in the craft knife and cut around the inked designs with a smooth motion. You will find that turning the mat instead of the knife will make the cuts smoother. If any ink remains along the cutout edges, remove it with a damp tissue so it does not mix with the paint in the first few uses.

Make a sample of the design before starting on the quilt. Use a piece of the same washed fabric as the quilt. If you are using paint or cream, use the dry-brush method. Put a small amount of paint in a shallow container. Hold the brush upright and dip just the tips into the paint. On a paper towel, work the brush in a circular motion until the paint is almost gone. In the beginning there will be little swirled lines on the paper. When these disappear and the color is soft and smooth, the brush is ready to be used on the fabric.

Work the brush in a circular motion away from the cut edge of the stencil to keep paint from seeping under the edge. To achieve shading, work more heavily in some areas. To set the color, follow the manufacturer's instructions.

To color an area with a stencil crayon, apply some color on the film around the edges of the part of the design to be worked. Use a clean brush and a circular motion to move the waxy paint onto the fabric. Shading can be added by working more heavily in some areas or by adding another color and blending it into the first.

This paint will feel dry almost immediately and does not need any special setting. However, because it is oil based and will not be really dry for about twenty-four hours, use care when continuing to put your quilt together.

Little Beauty on page 129 is a stenciled quilt. With the instructions is a reproduction of one of the squares colored with stencil crayons to highlight the look these paints give to our new quilts.

APPLIQUÉ ON MINIATURE QUILTS

Appliqué is an exciting medium when worked in miniature. The little pieces really show off the delicate stitching and design, making this a true art form.

There are many methods of applying appliqué pieces to a background fabric, and each of us who have tried various methods have several favorites. I remember seeing a class called "Thirteen Ways to Do Appliqué" advertised in a shop. Thinking about it on the way home, I did count that many ways to stitch decorative fabric to a background and I am sure that with some thought more could be added to the list. For miniatures some work better than others, so only those will be covered here. If you have a

(continued)

favorite that is not mentioned, use it by all means!

When choosing fabrics for appliqué, use the guidelines in the Basics section on page 138. Be very careful to choose tightly woven cottons since the edges need to be turned under in nice tight folds and it is best if the cut edges do not fray. Match the thread color to the appliqué pieces if possible and use as fine a cotton thread as can be found in the right color. Sometimes it is not possible to find exactly the right color. When that happens, opt for a shade a little darker than the appliqué and make the stitches as invisible as possible.

Easy Appliqué with Machine-Stitched Reinforced Edges

This method, which reinforces corners and curves and eliminates the need to try to hold a tiny piece in position while you stitch, was used for the little hearts, flowers, and leaves on the Romance hanging on page 41.

To work in this manner:

◆ Trace the motif onto typing paper or parchment and cut it out on the marked line.

◆ Place the papercut out on the appliqué fabric and trace around it with a wash-out marker. Stay as close to the edge of the paper as possible so the motif will not be larger than the pattern. Allow enough fabric for ¼" hems and if possible a little extra as shown in *Figure 1* to make the machine stitching in the following step easier.

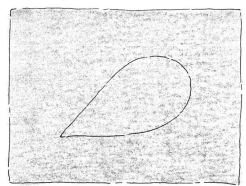

Figure 1

◆ With matching thread in your sewing machine, use a straight stitch about 1.5-mm long to stitch around the motif, placing the stitching on the drawn outline as shown in *Figure 2*. Begin and end the stitching on a long flat side if

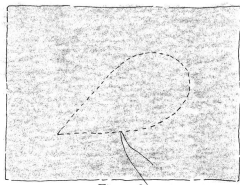

Figure 2

possible, as shown by the thread ends on the drawing.

◆ Pull the thread ends to the wrong side and cut off all but about ¼". Do not tie the ends. As you do the final stitching, tuck the ends under the appliqué so they do not show.

◆ Wash out the markings and press flat.

◆ Following the stitched outline, cut out the motif leaving a ⅛" seam

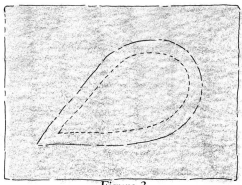

Figure 3

allowance as shown in **Figure 3**. This narrow seam allowance is all that is needed for an appliqué on a miniature quilt.

◆ Pin the cutout appliqué in position on the background fabric and hand-baste it, placing the basting stitches a generous ⅛" inside the machine stitching as shown in **Figure 4**.

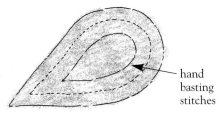

hand basting stitches

Figure 4

◆ Using the invisible appliqué stitch shown in **Figure 5**, and turning the hem under as you work, stitch the motif in place. As you

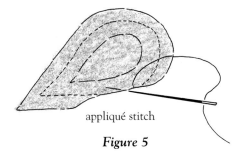

appliqué stitch

Figure 5

turn the hem back, roll the machine stitching to the underside so it does not show. If necessary, clip the hem to the stitching along curves to make it lie flat. As you begin stitching, it will be apparent that the hem allowance tucks into the space between the basting and the machine stitching on the edge.

◆ To do the appliqué stitch, bring the needle up from the wrong side through both the background and the appliqué as shown in Figure 5. (Again, it is easiest to begin and end the thread in a place like that shown on the drawing rather than at a point or curve.) Pull the thread through and continue in this manner.

Appliqué Using Freezer Paper

This is an excellent method when the pieces to be appliquéd are so small that the machine reinforcement stitching would be difficult. The freezer paper, which should be the wax-coated type, can be used on either side of the fabric, depending on the stitcher's preference.

Freezer Paper on the Right Side

◆ Trace the appliqué shape onto the non-shiny paper side of the freezer paper. Cut out the individual patterns.

◆ With the shiny side on the right side of the fabric, iron the shapes to the fabric.

◆ With the paper in place, and allowing ⅛" around the edges for the hem, cut out the motifs.

◆ Leaving the paper on the fabric, hold or pin the motifs in place. With the tip of the needle, turn under the hems as you stitch. There will be a very small edge along the paper into which to stitch.

Freezer Paper on Wrong Side

◆ Since in this technique the freezer paper is ironed to the wrong side of the fabric, the designs will be reversed unless you reverse the drawing before tracing it to the freezer paper. Simply trace the design on parchment, then turn it over and trace it through the paper. Cut out the shapes. Trace the shapes on the paper side of the freezer paper, then

(continued)

iron the shiny side to the wrong side of the fabric.

◆ Cut out the shapes allowing a ⅛" hem allowance beyond the edges of the freezer paper.

◆ Hold the motif in place and, with the tip of the needle, turn under the hem allowance as you stitch the motif in place. Stitch all the way around the piece, sealing the paper inside.

◆ Complete all the stitching on the piece. Make a little slit in the background fabric under each appliqué. Soak the piece in cool water for a few minutes. Roll in a towel to remove the excess water. Insert tweezers into the slits and remove the paper. It pulls out easily. Iron the piece to dry.

Stems, Bows, and Scrolls with Bias Tubing

Bias tubing makes narrow, vinelike motifs that curve and twist as you like. A bit of sewing machine preparation and the pieces are ready to stitch in place!

◆ Cut 1"-wide bias strips as instructed on page 152. Fold the bias strip in half lengthwise with right sides together as shown in **Figure 6**. To make a bias tubing that is ¼" wide, finished, place the stitching ¼" from the fold.

Figure 6

◆ Trim the seam allowance to a scant ¼". Cut one end of the strip at an angle as shown in Figure 6.

◆ Insert a loop turner through the tubing so the latch hook comes through at the angled end. Put the hook of the latch through the fabric at the longest point as shown in **Figure 7**.

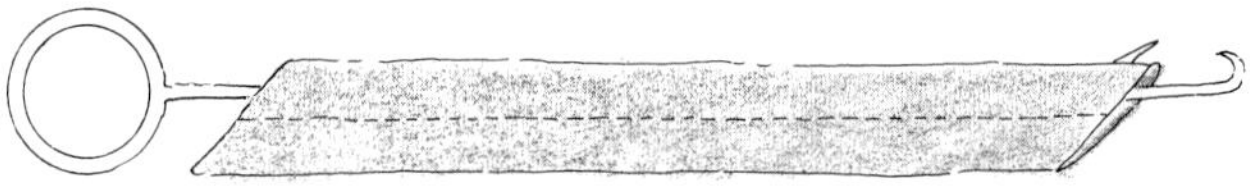

Figure 7

◆ Withdraw the turner, guiding it through the tubing with one hand and being careful not to pull hard enough to break the stitching. Turn

the tubing completely before removing the hook.

◆ Hold or pin the tubing in place on the background fabric and stitch along both sides to fasten in place.

Tubing with Seam Allowance on the Right Side

◆ Cut the bias strips as for the seamed tubing above.

◆ Fold the piece in half lengthwise with the right side out. For tubing ¼" wide, stitch ¼" from the fold.

◆ Trim the seam allowance to a scant ⅛". Press the tubing flat with the raw edge of the seam in the back.

◆ Holding the tubing so the raw edge is underneath, pin and stitch it in place. As with the other tubing, stitch both sides to the background fabric.